The Zodiac Decoded

by Joseph T. Cappa, Esq.

To All the Humans who are about to inherit this Earth

...notes from a casual observer

DORRANCE
PUBLISHING CO
EST. 1920
PITTSBURGH, PENNSYLVANIA 15238

Dorrance Publishing Co
585 Alpha Drive
Suite 103
Pittsburgh, PA 15238
Visit our website at *www.dorrancebookstore.com*

ISBN: 978-1-6495-7227-1
eISBN: 978-1-6495-7735-1

PREFACE

Welcome, Rainbow Generation, to the planet Earth! You have arrived at a most exciting time. Humanity is entering into a new age of development and understanding. It's a gigantic evolutionary leap forward, called the Age of Aquarius.

When I refer to the "Rainbow Generation," I am not only referring to the ever burgeoning LBGTQ+ community, whose prominence shall continue to blossom in the years to come. I am also referring to all the indigo children who have special talents, abilities, and/or sensibilities; all persons born on or after December 21, 2012; and every person of every race, creed, color, and manifestation under the sun, who question whether there is a grand design to this thing we call "life."

The arrival of the Rainbow Generation at the dawning of the Age of Aquarius is no coincidence. It was foretold in the stars of the zodiac long ago. I know this because I am one of the forerunners of the Rainbow Generation. I am a child of the 1960's. I arrived when the children of this planet started questioning the status quo and demanding change. We announced the dawning of the Age of Aquarius, envisioning a day when all humankind will live in harmony, and celebrated it with tie-dye, flower power, and love-ins. And at Woodstock, the young people in attendance held their candles high, so they could stay dry against the rain. It was truly magical.

I am not only a flower child of the 1960's, I also happen to be in the Aquarius phase of my own life. The days of wine, women, and song are over, and I now have to take stock in myself and take care of my body if I want to stay around. I realize that there is no one coming to save me or do it for me. I am responsible for my own life. I am the bearer of the waters of my own life, just as the Rainbow Generation will soon be the bearer of the waters of all life on this planet.

My role is to simply light a few candles to help guide your way while you embark on your epic journey to enjoy life; heal this planet; and carry us forward through the Age of Aquarius and eventually into the Age of Capricorn. Yes, my lovelies (too soon?), there is a bigger picture, a grand design if you will, and we are ALL a vital part of that grand design!

And who better to entrust this world to than a generation of people who realize that there is no "us versus them" anymore? There is only "us"; a generation of people who know to the very core of their being that all living things need and deserve love and respect. And it is the love of life, all life, that will ultimately save us. Yes (spoiler alert), love is the answer!

I have prepared the following literary work for your entertainment, education, and enlightenment. It is how we have known that the Rainbow Generation was coming at the dawning of the Age of Aquarius for quite some time now. Enjoy!

Joe Cappa (right now) TM

PART ONE
THE CIRCLE OF LIFE

My name is Joe Cappa. By profession, I am an attorney. However, by passion, I am a lover of knowledge. Ever since I was a young lad, I was obsessed with knowing the how's and why's of everything. My whole life, I obsessively challenged myself with daily puzzles and logic problems, to a point where I could solve even very difficult puzzles and logic problems without writing anything down. I graduated college with a major in Philosophy and went on to law school. Even after completing my law studies, I continued reading everything I could get my hands on in any and all possible subject matters. I wanted to be the wisest person on the planet… the ultimate philosopher! I literally read myself into poorer and poorer eyesight over the years. I guess you can say that I am one of those people who want to try to figure it all out before I go.

After some 30 years of doing logic problems and reading and absorbing as much as I could, I was quickly hitting middle age. I began to reflect more and more about my life. I began to review and grade my accomplishments and short-comings. I started to ask questions. Why are we all here? Is there a bigger picture to all of this? It is with these thoughts I began to look into the night sky. Star watching became my new hobby. I obtained a cell phone app that allowed me to see and identify all of the stars and constellations in the sky. It became a daily obsession.

Of all the stars to study, I became fixated on the stars of the zodiac. I not only looked up at the stars of the zodiac in the night sky, I could use the cell phone app to see the stars of the zodiac any time I wanted. It is with this background that I also began to do research as well. I found endless writings about many aspects of the zodiac; however, most of those writings are dedicated to astrology, horoscopes, and birth signs. Most of the remaining writings were on the scientific aspects of the zodiac stars. What I learned was that no one, absolutely no one, knew what the zodiac actually meant.

Why did the ancients create the zodiac? Why did they use the symbols they used and why are those symbols arranged in a certain order? There had to be a reason. It cannot be random. The zodiac symbols, in the order they were in, had to have a meaning that was known to all peoples long ago but somehow has been lost or forgotten over the ages. I decided to devote my studies to deciphering the zodiac. I finally had a purpose. I was determined to decipher the zodiac, and lo and behold, I did. I deciphered what the symbols of the zodiac actually mean.

It is important to note that when discussing the zodiac, I am in no way referring to what we commonly think of as astrology, horoscopes, birth signs, or how planetary alignments affect people, places, and things. I am strictly speaking of the 13 constellations that form a ring around the flat plane of our solar system that we call the zodiac. I believe it is easier to show you what I have discovered by walking you through the same steps I followed in deciphering the zodiac. This way, the reader can see for themselves, using their own knowledge and mind's eye, what the zodiac truly is. You will be able to see what the zodiac truly is for yourselves. No special training is needed.

First of all, what does the word "zodiac" mean? Most of us were taught that the word "zodiac" is a combination of two Greek words "zoa" and "diakos," meaning "circle of animals"; however, that is misleading. Not all of the characters are animals; some are people, two are mythical beasts, and one is an object. The word "zodiac" cannot mean "circle of animals." Some believe the word "zodiac" means the "circle of life," and yet others believe that the word "zodiac" means "circle of figurines."

My own investigation revealed that the "zo" in zodiac could mean either animals or life (in Greek "zoa" means "animals" and "zoe" means "life"). Since not all of the zodiac characters are animals, the "zo" in "zodiac" probably means "life." I further discovered that the word "diakos" does not mean "circle"; it means "exalted" or "revered." For example, Alexander the Great was considered "diakos." Although scholars do not agree on the exact definition of the word "zodiac," all agree that the word "zodiac" describes a circle of star groupings that form a belt or ring around the flat plane of our solar system.

My research has drawn me to the conclusion that the word "zodiac" actually means "circle of life" or "revered/exalted circle of life," and as such, it is, by definition, the story of us! The question then becomes, "How do I prove it to the reader?" Since I practice law, it occurred to me to present my case as if I was presenting evidence to a jury. I intend to let each reader act as a juror and determine for themselves, after reviewing all the evidence, whether the zodiac truly is the story of us.

I want each reader to make his or her own determination. I am confident that once you have reviewed all the evidence for yourselves, that you, the readers, will all agree that the zodiac is the "circle of life." I further believe that you will see that the zodiac's message applies to all of us. Each reader will come to understand what the zodiac truly is. It is the story of humanity written in the stars! It is the story of us!

In order to understand the zodiac's true meaning, you first must forget everything you think you already know about the zodiac. Forget birth signs, horoscopes, and astrology. Forget anything you have read or been taught by others. We need to relearn the zodiac together from scratch, and remove all the misconceptions. I believe the best way to start is to look at a diagram that gives the basic details of our solar system and the ring of stars that surround it that we call the zodiac.

The picture, below, is a very basic picture of the zodiac. The actual diagram would be much more complicated as it would have to account for the Earth's seasonal rotation on its axis and things like that. For our purposes however, the picture below provides all of the information we need.

From looking at the above picture, we can learn a lot of facts. We can see, with our very own eyes, that the Earth (and moon and visible planets) all travel around the sun on a flat plane. We call this flat plane the "ecliptic." Surrounding this ecliptic plane are the stars of the zodiac. They seem to form a belt or ring around our solar system, and from our view here on Earth, the sun, moon, and other planets appear to be traveling in front of (eclipsing) the stars of the zodiac at all times.

We can see that from our viewpoint here on Earth, that the sun appears to move in a complete counterclockwise circle each year. In reality, it is the Earth that is moving. However, from our vantage point, it appears as if the sun is moving, and we are standing still. Each year, the sun appears to pass in front of all of the zodiac constellations and returns to its beginning point. As you can see from the picture, in March, when you look up at the sun, it is front of Pisces. In April, it is front of Aries. In May, it is in front of Taurus. These are approximations, because although the months and zodiac symbols used to match up exactly once upon a time, over time things have changed.

Following the sun on its annual counterclockwise path through the zodiac constellations is where we get our calendar and our basic understanding of astrology, birth signs, and horoscopes. However, looking at this picture, four things should become immediately apparent to the viewer, all of which are vital in deciphering the zodiac:

1. The zodiac and our annual calendar form a counterclockwise circle. From our vantage point here on Earth the months and zodiac symbols as we familiarly know them (Aquarius, Pisces, Aries, Taurus, etc.) actually form a counter-clockwise circle around our solar system. Look at the picture again, and see for yourselves how the zodiac symbols and the months of our calendar form a counterclockwise circle. March is actually at 9:00 on a circular calendar, and September is at 3:00. We have been drawing our analog calendars backwards since the "dark" ages. This may be one of the reasons the true meaning of the zodiac has been lost.

    If the zodiac is not just some random ring of characters, if the zodiac is to have meaning, such as the symbols are to form a story told in a series of pictures, then perhaps we should proceed in a clockwise circle in our sky (backwards or inverse from the way we normally follow the zodiac). Just like a comic strip or the writing on the top of a coin, we should always go from left to right or in a clockwise circle. We will leave this point for now, but remember, if the zodiac is to have meaning, then we should be going in a clockwise circle through the zodiac (in inverse order from the way we normally associate the zodiac symbols). What if the zodiac is supposed to be read from left to right?

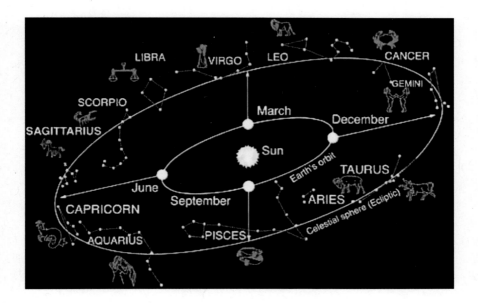

2. <u>The zodiac pictures look nothing like the star patterns they are assigned to</u>. For example, Aries the Ram is four stars in almost a straight line. How do you get a ram out of four stars in a straight line? The constellation Capricornus the Sea-Goat is actually an upside-down triangle of stars. How do you get a sea-goat from an upside-down triangle? Look at the picture below, you can see for yourselves that the star patterns do not actually look like the characters that are assigned to them.

    What this means is that the zodiac symbols have a meaning that have nothing to do with what the star patterns actually look like. They could have drawn any characters they wanted in any of the star groupings but chose to draw the characters they did, in the order they did, for a reason. It is not a random list of characters. I suggest to you that the stars of the constellation Aries the Ram could have been any design, and it would still be called the "ram." The same applies to all of the zodiac symbols. The stars and characters do not match each other, which means that the zodiac symbols have a meaning independent of what the star patterns actually look like. They must have used the symbols they used, and put those symbols in a certain order for a reason. What if each of the zodiac symbols was actually a picture, and all the pictures added together, in the order they are in, form a story… something we call a "pictograph"?

3. <u>There are 13 constellations of the zodiac.</u> Most people do not know this; however, there are actually thirteen constellations in the zodiac. The one that most people never heard of is the Constellation Ophiuchus, the Serpent Bearer. This word is pronounced "oh-fee-you-kus". This constellation is a man, standing and holding a snake.

There are a number of reasons that this constellation is ignored when depicting the modern zodiac; however, the basic reason is that it occupies the same one-twelfth of the circle as Scorpius, so when the zodiac was broken down into 12 equal parts, Ophiuchus was simply left out. Look at the first picture again. It shows where Ophiuchus sits in the zodiac ring. As you will see, it sits right in between Scorpius and Sagittarius. Only the foot of Ophiuchus touches the ecliptic plane. That, and the fact that it occupies the same one-twelfth of the circle as another constellation (Scorpius), are two basic reasons Ophiuchus is overlooked when breaking the zodiac down into twelve equal parts.

As you will soon see for yourselves, we need all 13 constellations of the zodiac in order to decipher its true meaning. Perhaps each zodiac symbol is like a chapter in a story….and this story has 13 chapters.

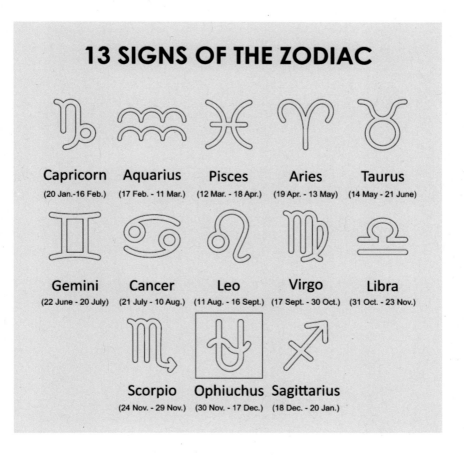

13 SIGNS OF THE ZODIAC

Capricorn
(20 Jan.-16 Feb.)

Aquarius
(17 Feb. - 11 Mar.)

Pisces
(12 Mar. - 18 Apr.)

Aries
(19 Apr. - 13 May)

Taurus
(14 May - 21 June)

Gemini
(22 June - 20 July)

Cancer
(21 July - 10 Aug.)

Leo
(11 Aug. - 16 Sept.)

Virgo
(17 Sept. - 30 Oct.)

Libra
(31 Oct. - 23 Nov.)

Scorpio
(24 Nov. - 29 Nov.)

Ophiuchus
(30 Nov. - 17 Dec.)

Sagittarius
(18 Dec. - 20 Jan.)

4.   <u>Although the word "zodiac" is Greek in origin and all of the con-</u>
     <u>stellation names are either Greek or Roman, the zodiac is thou-</u>
     <u>sands of years older than the Greeks and Romans, so the true</u>
     <u>meaning of the zodiac has nothing to do with Greek or Roman</u>
     <u>mythology. The zodiac is also thousands of years older than the</u>
     <u>Babylonian Empire, so it has nothing to do with modern astrol-</u>
     <u>ogy, which was invented by the Babylonians, **thousands of years**</u>
     <u>**after** the zodiac was first created.</u>

     Although most of what we know about the zodiac comes from
the Greeks and Romans, the zodiac existed for thousands of years
before either of these cultures arose. Archeologists have traced
the zodiac all the way back to the Sumerians, who were deemed
to be the first modern human civilization (approx. 4,000 BCE-
2,000 BCE). It was the Sumerians who gave us the 13 constellations of the zodiac. The symbols did not have the Greek names
we associate with them today; however, the underlying symbols
of the zodiac have been the same, in the same order, since first
created by the Sumerians. For example, there was no "Aries the
Ram"; it was just the symbol for "ram." It was not "Taurus the
Bull"; it was just the symbol for "bull." The same applies to all
the zodiac symbols.

Sumerian Cuneiform Alphabet

The Sumerian clay tablets tell us that they learned mathematics, science, and astronomy from the Anunnaki, who they describe as god-like peoples, who came down from above the clouds (mountains) and taught civilization basics to the Sumerians. For example, the basis for our modern measurement of time and angles came from the Sumerians, who claim the Anunnak taught it to them.

If you hold up the four fingers of one hand and count the three sections of each finger, altogether you will count to 12. If you also hold up all five of the fingers of the other hand you get the basis of our measurement system. Twelve times five is 60. This is where we get 60 seconds in a minute and 60 minutes in an hour. It is also where we get an analog clock face with 12 sections, each with five minutes in it. This numbering system is also where we get 360 degrees in a circle. It is also why you only need one-sixth of a circle (60 degrees) to define the whole circle.

What does this mean? It means that what the Anunnaki taught the Sumerians is very important indeed. Much of what the Anunnaki taught the Sumerians is still used in modern civilization to this very day. Perhaps it was the Anunnaki who taught the zodiac to the Sumerians.

[Interesting side note: The total number of fingers that you are holding up is nine, and all of the angles of our basic Platonic solids (and natural rhythmic frequencies) always add up to nine. For example, 180 degrees in a triangle...one plus eight is nine. There are 360 degrees in a square and circle...three plus six is nine, etc. In addition, the natural resonant frequency of the universe is 432Hz, and those three numbers add up to nine.]

After the collapse of the Sumerian Empire, the zodiac lay dormant until it was adopted by the Babylonians (approx. 1,800 BCE - 624 BCE). To the Babylonians, the Sumerians were considered "ancient peoples." The Babylonians broke down the zodiac into a wheel containing 12 equal sections (omitting Ophiuchus). They matched the calendar with the zodiac which gave us our modern 12-month calendar. It was also the Babylonians who did all the measurements and mathematics that gave rise to modern astrology, birth signs, and horoscopes. (They could do a lot of math and measurements using 12 that they could not do using 13.)

It is during this time that the zodiac seemed to spread throughout the known world. The 12-part zodiac wheel has been found in just about every culture surrounding Mesopotamia where it was first created. Archeologists have found the zodiac wheel as far East as India. There are other cultures around the world who have their own zodiac; however, they are beyond the scope of this writing.

Following the decline of the Babylonian Empire, the zodiac again lay dormant until around 330 BCE when Alexander the Great conquered the known world, including the former Babylonian Empire. It is said that Alexander the Great discovered the zodiac in the Babylonian ruins and had it brought back to Greece. From there, the Greeks revived the zodiac and put their own spin on it. They added their own legends and mythologies to the zodiac, as did the Romans thereafter.

What does this mean? It means that the zodiac has been with us since the very beginning of modern civilization and was probably something that all peoples of the time understood. It also means that the zodiac has an original meaning that had nothing to do with modern astrology or mythology.

If looking for the true meaning of the zodiac one should look to the symbols assigned by the Sumerians, not the Greek or Roman names. Remember, the symbols have been the same, in the same order, since the zodiac was first created. For our purposes, however, I will still use the Greek and Roman names that we are all familiar with to make it easier to follow along.

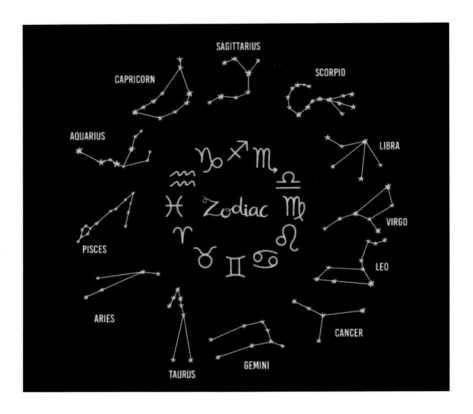

What we have learned thus far is that the zodiac has been with us from the beginning of modern civilization. It has the same symbols in the same order since it was first created. It has nothing to do with astrology or mythology. The zodiac symbols do not look like the star patterns they are assigned to. There are 13 constellations in the zodiac. We learned that the word "zodiac" means "circle of life," not "circle of animals." We also learned that the zodiac, in the order we familiarly reference it, is actually forming a counter-clockwise band around the perimeter of our solar system.

It was at that point when it occurred to me to list the zodiac symbols as they appear clockwise across our sky and below is what the list looks like:

> The Sea-Goat (Capricornus)
> The Hunter (Sagittarius)
> The Serpent Bearer (Ophiuchus)
> The Scorpion (Scorpius)
> The Scales (Libra)
> The Maiden (Virgo)
> The Lion (Leo)
> The Crab (Cancer)
> The Lovers (Gemini)
> The Bull (Taurus)
> The Ram (Aries)
> The Fish (Pisces)
> The Water Bearer (Aquarius)
> The Sea-Goat (Capricornus)

Please note that I started with Capricornus the Sea Goat simply because it was at the top of the picture I was looking at. I also noted that when the modern zodiac was formalized, Capricornus was the constellation behind the sun when it got to the shortest day of the year (12/21) and then when the days start getting longer again (12/25). The Constellation Capricornus therefore has been associated with the end and beginning of the sun's annual cycle. I therefore put Capricornus at the beginning and the end of the list, just to see how it looks.

As I stood there looking at this list the thought occurred to me… Perhaps Capricornus is a mythological creature representing birth and death. Remember, the word "zodiac" means "circle of life." What if the half goat-half fish symbol, which is known as the "water creature that becomes a land animal" and also known as "the intelligent creature (goat) that can navigate the waters of life (fish)" is actually describing a newborn who, in fact, is an intelligent creature that has gone from the waters of the womb and took a magical journey to become a land animal. The newborn is also described as the "intelligent creature that has successfully navigated the waters of life," which is the same definition as the Sea-Goat. It appears that Capricornus the Sea-Goat does indeed describe birth/the newborn of all mammals.

I further noted that at the end of life, we once again navigate the waters of life, this time from life to death. It occurred to me that the Sea-Goat (Capricornus) must not only represent birth, it must also represent death or, in terms of stages of life, newborn and senior citizen. I therefore kept the Sea-Goat (Capricornus) at the beginning and end of my list. Altogether, we now have 14 symbols in the list.

If Capricornus the Sea-Goat represents birth and death, then the other symbols of the zodiac (circle of life) may be the various stages of life that we all go through between birth and death. This is where it hit me. The symbols of the zodiac, which means "circle of life," **must** be pictorial representations of the stages of life. So, the next thing I did was research to see what the recognized stages of life are. I would write down a list of the stages of life and compare it to the list of zodiac symbols (in clockwise order) and see if I find a matching pattern.

The stages of life turn out to have exactly 14 stages with the first and last being birth/newborn and senior citizen/death. The list looks like this:

0 - Birth/newborn
1 - Crawling teething infant
1 - Walking/talking toddler
2 - Terrible twos
3 - Measuring child
5 - Introduction to society/school
8 - Beginning social activities
13 - Teenager
21 - Marriage
21+ - New parents
21++ - Parents of toddlers
34 - Raising a family in a community
55 - Mid-life/middle age
?? - Senior citizen/death/rebirth

The recognized stages of life have been the same ever since the beginning of humanity. We still celebrate all of these stages of life to this very day. Each of the stages in the life cycle of a human being is well documented. Look at the list again! Each reader may recall having gone through each of these stages during their own life or witnessed others, like their own children, going through these exact stages, in this exact order. One need only use their own experiences and their own mind's eye to see each of the chapters of this story for themselves. No special training or education is required.

I first noted that the stages of life follow the Fibonacci sequence almost exactly, especially in the early years. The Fibonacci sequence is the pattern of growth for many biological organisms on the planet Earth. This same growth pattern is found throughout nature and the cosmos, and it is the basic math behind a spiraling pattern. The sequence goes as follows: First you have the numbers "zero" and "one". Then, you add those two numbers together and get the number "one". Add one plus one and you get "two." Add one plus two, and you get "three." Add two plus three, and you get "five." Add three plus five, and you get "eight." Add five plus eight, and you get "13," and so on [0,1,1,2,3,5,8,13,21...].

Humans grow along the Fibonacci sequence, just as many living things do. Our stages of life develop along the Fibonacci sequence, almost exactly, year by year, especially in the early years. For example, we are born at "0". By the age of one, we have become crawling, teething infants. Shortly thereafter, also around the age of one, we become walking, talking toddlers. At age two, we enter the "terrible twos." At age three, we become the "measuring child." By age five, the child begins its social life, brand new fresh and innocent. (0,1,1,2,3,5…) If I am seeing the pattern correctly, the zodiac symbols will match up to the stages of life, in order, exactly,

Next to the list of the stages of life, I began to write down the zodiac symbols and their description. Please note that I started and ended with Capricornus. Just like in mathematics, you need at least one-sixth of the circle to match exactly in order to define the whole circle (remember the Sumerians). With that in mind, I began to look to see if I can find at least three matches in a row (three symbols in a row out of 14 gives us more than one-sixth of the circle).

As I scanned the list, I immediately noticed that next to the terrible twos was a scorpion. I noted that both the scorpion and the toddler screaming at its parent, both strike out in attack. They match. I noted that the very next stage of life was the measuring child and next to it was the zodiac symbol "scales"… both measure. Another exact match. I then noted that the next stage of life is "introduction into society, brand new, fresh and innocent" and next to it is the zodiac symbol "maiden/virgin"…"brand new, fresh and innocent". Again, they match exactly. We now have three symbols in a row that match the stages of life exactly, in order. We can now define the entire circle.

I completed the list and here is what it looks like:

		Zodiac = The Circle of Life	
Age	**Stage of Life**	**Description**	**Symbol**
0	Birth/Rebirth	water creature becomes land animal can/has navigated the waters of life	Capricornus (the sea goat)
1	Crawling, teething infant	child races around on all fours smashes and eats everything it catches	Sagittarius (the hunter)
1	Toddler	walks and talks carries around objects of its desire	Ophiuchus serpent bearer
2	Terrible Twos	sharp stinging words of separation "NO!' 'ME!" "MINE!'	Scorpius (the scorpion)
3	Measuring/Counting Child	child learns to count and compare measures and labels things	Libra (the scales)
5	Introduction to society (school)	start of school and its social life brand new, fresh and innocent	Virgo (the maiden)
8	Begin social activities sports, religious training	lets its hair down, kings of their jungle travels around in a "pack" of friends	Leo (the lion)
13	Teenager declared an adult danger years	learns the outside world for themselves beware dangers lurking in waters of life	Cancer (the crab)
21	Marriage merging	child takes on a mate and starts their own household. Fresh new lifestyle	Gemini (lovers)
21+	Having infant children (enforced practices)	new parents lives centered on the baby scheduled needs, rules and discipline	Taurus (the bull)
21++	Parents of toddler (follow the rules)	set up a reward based system of rules negotiating with toddlers	Aries (the ram)
21+++	Family in a community (school of fish)	doing what families do doing things in kid's same age group	Pisces (the fish)
midlife	Middle age midlife crisis	no one coming to save me wine women song become yoga & exer. become the bearer of waters of 1"s life	Aquarius (water bearer)
Senior Citizen	Senior citizen death and rebirth	intelligent creatures that can navigate the waters of life; (ie) retirees death and rebirth	Capricornus (the seat goat)

Do you see the pattern? All, not some, <u>ALL</u> of the zodiac symbols match a corresponding stage of life. The 14 zodiac symbols describe the 14 stages of life, in exact order!

Follow along with me as we re-discover the true meaning of the zodiac for ourselves:

CAPRICORNUS, THE SEA GOAT

(age birth to newborn)

Capricorn

The sea goat is the back half of a fish and front half of a goat. It is the water creature that becomes a land animal. It is also known as the intelligent creature that can navigate the waters of life. The unborn goes from the waters of the womb and emerges at birth as a land animal, already knowing how to feed itself. As the zodiac symbol describes, the newborn is the water creature that emerges as the intelligent land animal. Put another way, the newborn is the intelligent creature that has successfully navigated the waters of life, just like the mythological creature, Capricornus, the Sea Goat.

Every culture celebrates birth. Not only do humans celebrate birth, all sentient beings celebrate birth. Every parent can recall the birth of their children. The strange looking creature that emerged from their mother's womb, all wet and wrinkly from their lives in the waters of the amniotic sac. Birth is always signaled by the mom's "water breaking." I can still recall with excitement when my wife announced to me that her water had broken. I knew that it meant that the creature in her belly was soon to be born.

As soon as the newborn emerges from its mother's womb, it lets out a lung clearing cry that sounds strangely like that of a small animal, perhaps a baby goat. Soon thereafter the newborn demonstrates the ability to root and suckle. It is only moments old, and yet it knows how to turn its mouth to the food source and then latch on and feed itself. Every mother can recall vividly watching their newborn find the food source and immediately start to feed itself for the first time. Every mother has experienced, firsthand, the water creature emerging as the intelligent land animal. Everyone who has ever held a new-born has personally met the intelligent creature that had just successfully navigated the waters of life.

As every animal, including humans, start their lives on this planet as new-borns, the zodiac symbol representing birth in animal form therefore makes perfect sense. The use of parts of a goat and a fish are a perfect illustration of the intelligent creature (goat) that can navigate the waters of life (fish). Every human and every mammal ever born on this planet, has been, for a brief instant, a newborn…CAPRICORNUS, THE SEA-GOAT.

SAGITTARIUS, THE HUNTER

(age ~1; crawling/teething infant)

Sagittarius

At this age, the child has mastered crawling and is teething. The child is always racing off on all fours exploring its immediate environment, and it puts <u>every-thing</u> and <u>anything</u> it catches while "hunting" in its mouth. You have to "child proof" your house, or the little creature will get its hands on everything it can and will either destroy what it catches and/or try to eat it. Remember, it's teething, and everything it catches goes into its mouth.

Every parent or babysitter can recall having chased a crawling infant through the house, where the child grabs onto everything it can get its hands on. Parents can recall having child-proofed their house to protect their valuables. We can all recall watching a baby knock over cups and/or clear off a coffee table in a matter of seconds. We can all recall having stopped a baby from eating carpet fuzz, dog food, mommy's hair, and even its own dirty hands. We can all recall having to grab a pacifier or frozen chew toy to satisfy their child's teething pain.

If you have ever chased a crawling infant while it is off exploring its surroundings, grabbing at, tearing, smashing, and putting everything it gets its hands on into its mouth, then you have encountered "the hunter." Not only do human children go through this phase, so do dogs, cats, and all other mammals. Anyone who has ever raised a litter or owned a kitten or puppy has witnessed the animal go from thing to thing, pouncing and chewing on anything they can get to, as they are teething and learning to master their immediate environments. It is during this stage that the mammal practices its primeval hunting skills, pouncing, tearing, chewing, etc. It is a fact of life. All mammals go through the "hunter" phase, practicing their inherited skills, shortly after birth.

The zodiac symbol of part man, part horse, holding a bow and arrow, is a perfect illustration of man (and animals) going through the hunter phase in the early part of their lives. Every person reading this right now all now know that they spent a part of their early lives as SAGITTARIUS, THE HUNTER.

OPHIUCHUS, THE SERPENT BEARER

(age ~1; walking, talking toddler)

Ophiuchus

This word is pronounced "oh-fee-you-kus." This constellation is traditionally ignored in favor of Scorpius when discussing the zodiac signs (molded into the perfect number "12"), but it is a distinctly separate developmental stage in human life, hence its inclusion in the zodiac.

The child learns to walk and talk. The toddler can now communicate with others through spoken language (has control of its tongue…the serpent). The child also now has hands free while moving to grasp, climb, hold onto and carry away objects of its desire, like a favorite toy, "baba," or mommy's cell phone. The objects of the toddler's desire, including its own tongue/spoken word, are the serpent.

Every parent can recall their child standing in front of them babbling in their own unique language, as if they were having a real conversation. Every parent has a picture of their toddler standing there and either sucking their thumb or drinking from a "baba" with one hand, while holding a favorite toy or "blankie" in its other hand. The child is so proud, standing there with the objects of its desire in its hands, just like the constellation picture.

The symbol is a man, standing, and proudly holding a snake. It is a perfect illustration of the human, standing and in control of its own tongue. If you have witnessed a toddler asking for and then carrying around a favorite toy, "baba" or "blankie," you have encountered OPHIUCHUS, THE SERPENT BEARER.

SCORPIUS, THE SCORPION

(age ~2; terrible twos)

Scorpio

In modern times, we call this stage the "terrible twos." The parents are toilet training the child at this stage. The child's eating, sleeping, dressing, playing, and toilet training are regimented by the parents on strict schedules, and the child is often being physically manipulated over and over again. This is where the child first pulls away from its parents' unconditional love to form its own identity. This stage is marked by sharp, stinging words of separation such as "NO!", "ME!", and "MINE!" When you think of a scorpion striking out with its stinger, think of a child in the midst of the terrible twos yelling at his or her parents with sharp, stinging words.

Every parent can vividly recall their children going through this phase, where the child screams "NO!" to anything and everything they are offered. The child, at times, just wants to be left alone and may be inconsolable.

It is no surprise that the zodiac recognizes this phase, as every parent will go through this phase with their children. Not only do modern humans go through this stage, mothers have endured going through the terrible twos phase with each of their children ever since humanity started. It is just a fact of life and has been recognized since the beginning of humanity. We all took our turns in life acting like the scorpion.

In addition, the parents are apt to be under unprecedented stresses, including loss of sleep, and may even occasionally strike out at each other, like scorpions. It is an unavoidable fact of life and has been this way ever since humanity began.

When you think of a child first striking out to form its own identity, sometimes with sharp, stinging words, think of SCORPIUS, THE SCORPION.

LIBRA, THE SCALES

(age ~3; measuring/counting child)

Libra

By the age of three, the child begins to count and measure things, and compare itself to others in their world, such as siblings and other family members. For example, the child now knows that three cookies are better than two and knows its place in the "pecking order" of its immediate family. All of us can recall having witnessed a child using their fingers to show you how old they are. By this age, they all learn to hold up three fingers! This phase of life is known as the "measuring/counting child."

Every parent can recall their children at this phase. The child is learning their colors, letters and numbers. The child repeats everything and is learning at an astounding rate. Every parent has used their own fingers to demonstrate the numbers "one," "two," and "three" to their child at this age. Ask any child at this age how old they are, and they will hold up a number of fingers. They are "this many" years old.

The child is not only repeatedly asking "what's that?" many times a day, it is also naming things and learning letters, numbers, and colors. In addition, the child can now compare and choose things. Children at this stage all know that more is better than less when it comes to goodies. If given a choice, the child at this age knows to choose the stack that has more cookies in it.

In addition to the above, the child now knows its place in the pecking order of the family. It knows that it ranks below the older siblings but higher than the family dog and younger siblings. It recognizes family and friends, becomes fearful of strangers, and is always testing itself against the status quo.

Many children at this stage have begun making order out of their world and will insist on doing things their way, or the way that makes sense to them. Every parent can remember having discussion with their toddler as to why the child should do something (like take a nap) or not do something (like take another's toy from them) with the child reasoning differently for their desired result. Every parent can recall having negotiated with their child during in this phase. It is a fact of life and has been ever since the beginning of humanity.

When you think of a child counting and measuring things and comparing itself to the world around it, think of a scale…LIBRA, THE SCALES.

VIRGO, THE MAIDEN/VIRGIN

(age ~5; introduction to society – school)

Virgo

At this stage, the child is first introduced to society. The child enters school and begins its social life. It establishes its first social identity and takes its place in the hierarchy of the social structure, brand new, fresh and innocent.

Every parent can recall their child's first day of school. Many parents even take pictures of the child all dressed up and ready for his or her first day. Every parent can also remember that happy yet tear-shedding moment when their child walks into the school on their first day to start their social life. This can be a very traumatic experience for the parents and the child.

The zodiac symbol of a maiden/virgin, brand new, fresh, and innocent, perfectly illustrates one's introduction into society. We all started our social lives when we started school. We were all fresh, brand new, and innocent, just starting our social life.

Every parent who shed a tear as they watched their child enter their first day of school to start their social life has personally shed a tear for VIRGO, THE MAIDEN/ VIRGIN.

LEO, THE LION

(age ~8; start of social activities)

Leo

At this stage, the child lets its hair grow out (the lion's mane). The child starts formal religious training, youth sports, social clubs, and related activities. It explores and conquers its domain, establishes itself among friends and peers, and is mastering its ever-growing social environment. They are the kings of their jungle during this phase of life.

Every parent can recall having a carload of kids of this age, acting up and laughing together as you drove them to soccer practice or other social activities. The kids are pumped up and full of themselves. They travel around with their "pack" of friends and learn the value of group dynamics for themselves.

The zodiac symbol of a lion with full mane perfectly illustrates the child, with its hair (mane) grown out, traveling in a "pack or pride" of friends, all doing things together. They are kings of their jungle at this phase. What perfect representation of "kings of their jungle" than the true king of the jungle, a male lion.

Any parent who played the role of soccer mom/dad can vividly recall their children acting like kings of their jungle at this age. This is LEO, THE LION.

CANCER, THE CRAB

Cancer

It is in the teenage years that the child learns of the outside world for itself for the first time. Teenage children experiment with sex, alcohol, drugs, and perhaps unwise stunts or endeavors during these "danger" years. We all know of children who did not survive this phase of life due to drunk driving accidents and overdoses, or did other things that could deny, hamper, or severely limit their future growth, such as, teenage pregnancies, criminal records, etc. Teenagers testing the waters of life on their own for the first time must beware the dangers lurking in the waters of life.

Every parent can recall their child entering this phase. We have many religious ceremonies around the globe, celebrating the child entering this phase of their lives where the child is deemed an adult and is now responsible for his or her own actions. We imbue them with a sense of self responsibility in hopes that they will be careful as they discover the outside world for themselves for the first time. We can also recall having heard of horror and tragedy of those who were unable to beware the dangers lurking in the waters of life.

The zodiac symbol of a crab is a perfect illustration that all people could understand. If you ever stepped on a crab while walking barefoot through murky waters, you know all too well to beware the dangers lurking in the waters of life. If you step on a crab, you will be pinched, it will hurt, you will go spastic, jump, scream, and run away. When learning the outside world on your own during your teenage years, you must beware the dangers lurking in the waters of life, just like you must be careful not to step on a crab.

Any parent who has ever worried about their teenage children being out of the family fold, unsupervised, has worried for the dangers their child might encounter. Every teenager testing the waters of life on their own, must be mindful to beware the dangers lurking in the waters of life... CANCER, THE CRAB.

GEMINI, THE LOVERS

(age ~21; marriage)

Gemini

At this stage, the child is formally an adult. It moves out on its own, makes its own home, and takes a mate. Together, they form a new life and family of their own. The individual, now merged with a partner, creates their own entity and make their own rules, folklore, ethos, and living environments in which to start their own family.

Most children will leave the family nest one day. Many of us can recall either moving out on our own and/or recall their children moving out on their own for the first time. The parents are always busy buying furniture and other knick-knacks for their child's new home. The child in forming its new domain makes all his or her own house rules and creates their own living conditions.

It is during this stage that the young adult takes on a mate with which to form their own family. There is a merging of families, which is celebrated as marriage and, in modern times, a civil union. Every person who has taken a mate and every parent who has attended and/or paid for a wedding can vividly recall their child entering the Gemini phase of their lives. Merging with another to create your own family is the GEMINI, THE LOVERS stage of life.

The zodiac symbol of two lovers entwined perfectly illustrates the marriage/ merging phase of life…two persons forming one entity. The symbol is self-explanatory. Even persons who do not marry but engage their careers, hobbies, etc., enter this phase.

TAURUS, THE BULL

(age ~21+; new parents)

Taurus

Once parents have a newborn infant, they need to be regimented, with strict rules, schedules, procedures and practices to attend to their newborn child's sleeping, feeding, changing, learning and other needs. The new parents dictate the rules and physically manipulate the child (dressing, feeding, changing diapers, etc.), and their infant has no choice but to do as mandated.

Every parent can remember the first few months of their infant's lives filled with schedules and rules. For example, the child must be fed every few hours just a certain amount of formula. Feeding is followed by burping and then changing and then back to bed until the next feeding. It is a crazy time for all, and each parent can vividly recall having been in "the rule" phase of their lives, where their entire lives were completely wrapped around the infant's "scheduled needs," requiring strict adherence to the rules. If a parent fails to follow such rules, the parent will suffer a crying or hungry or tired, or whatever, infant. In this phase, one must follow the rules in order for things to go smoothly.

We can also see this strict "rule" based behavior in persons who did not have children but instead may have adopted a pet, purchased a home or car, or even purchased house plants. At first, there are strict rules associated with the new house, pet, car, etc. For example, "In my house we take our shoes off," etc.

Please note that as the child grows and enters into the toddler phase, the parents will slowly start transitioning to the next "parent" phase. Parents who are too strict in the Taurus stage of their lives who fail to transition into the next "Aries" stage can cause severe problems with the development/psyche of their children, because the overly strict regimen thwarts the child's exploring or independence seeking phases of their own lives. There is a direct correlation between psychological problems in children related to traumas, real or imagined, suffered at the hands of parents who were overly strict in the "Taurus" phase of their own lives. Apparently, the zodiac has given us a wise lesson here! As the children go through the stages of their lives, the parents must be flexible and also transition from stage to stage or else there could be problems down the line.

The use of a bull to represent this stage of life is clear. We have all heard the expression "stubborn as a bull," as bulls are known to be inflexible. When dealing with a bull, one must adhere to repetitive, strict, safe practices to avoid danger. Structure, order and routine are required. New parents similarly are required to follow strict schedules to attend to their infant's needs. During this phase of life, strict adherence to rules, structure, and schedules are foremost in the new parents' minds.

New parents, ruling themselves, their families, and infant children with strict, regimented practices is the TAURUS THE BULL stage.

ARIES, THE RAM

(age ~21++; parents of toddlers)

Aries

As the individual's children grow and establish their own identities, the old "inflexible rule" phase begins to fade, and parents are forced into a new paradigm. Although some rules remain steadfast, parents are now required to allow the children to celebrate life as they please, as long as their children follow the rules. For example, "Finish your vegetables, and you can have dessert"; "Pick up your toys, and you can go out and play." The emphasis on strict unbreakable regimen gives way to granted freedoms to the child, as long as they follow the rules.

It is at this phase of life where the toddler begins to negotiate the rules. It is also where parents are sometimes forced to negotiate with their toddler to get them to do what the parents want them to do, like take a nap. Negotiating with toddlers is a fact of life that every parent will go through and has been a fact of life ever since humanity began.

Every parent can recall telling their children to follow the rules, and they can have a reward. It is just a fact of life. The child is reaching stages of independence, and by doing as expected of them, the child is granted certain privileges/rewards. All children learn to follow the rules, and as long as they follow the rules, their granted freedoms multiply. All parents can also recall having negotiated with their toddler or have their toddler negotiate the rules with them. Negotiating and a reward system signal this stage of life.

The use of a ram as the symbol for this stage of life is clear. Just as a ram must be exact in its footing to climb to the top of a hill or mountain, the toddler must follow the rules in order to get what or where they want. Just as a ram must negotiate the face of a steep mountain, toddlers learn to negotiate the rules with their parents, and the parents are now required to negotiate with their toddlers.

Similarly, as a ram must lovingly attend its flock, allowing the members of its fold to do their own "thing" as long as they follow the ram's basic rules; the parent of a toddler must allow their child the freedom to explore and establish themselves, as long as they follow the parents' basic rules.

Parents of toddlers, making rules and requiring children to voluntarily follow them, with a degree of negotiation both ways, is the ARIES THE RAM stage.

PISCES, THE FISH

(age ~34; mates raising a family in a community)

Pisces

At this stage, the offspring are in school and the individual and mate are busy raising their family, practicing their chosen profession(s) and interacting daily in the social environment around them, particularly as it relates to their children. At this stage, the parents and family are part of a much larger "school of fish," all basically doing the same as the others in the same stage.

This is the basic formula for raising a family in a community. The family is part of a larger social group, doing things like all the other community members who have children the same age. We work at our professions, take our kids to school and to after school activities. We attend each other's functions, like birthday parties and religious and sporting events. We are coaches or members of the PTA or some other local civic groups that help the schools and community function. We are doing things as a family just like all other families with children in the same age groups. It's just us, doing as we do as a family, during this stage of life.

We are so busy wrapped up in this part of our lives that it seems to pass by all too quickly. Before you know it, 10 years have gone behind you, and your kids are moving off to college or moving out on their own.

The use of two fish to represent this stage of life is clear. The two fish (parents) are acting as part of a much larger group (school of fish). When you think of you and your mate raising a family, acting as an integral part of the community around them, like fish in a larger school of fish, think of PISCES, THE FISH.

AQUARIUS, THE WATER BEARER

(age ~55; mid-life/middle-age)

Aquarius

Having reached middle age, the individual is no longer a part of the social groups that had governed their lives in the last stage. They are facing life changing issues, like being empty nesters, loss of job, or health related issues, etc. The individual must now take stock of itself. They are required to start taking care of their bodies and come to the realization that no one else can take care of them but themselves. It's up to them.

Although it sounds like a noble endeavor, most people do not change unless they have to. Something happens in their life that makes them change. People at this stage are faced with life changing issues and/or are sick and tired of doing the things that make them sick and tired. In modern times, we acknowledge this as a "midlife crisis." It is at this stage that the individual must re-invent themselves; however, this time in a healthier, more positive ethos. Wine, women, and song are replaced with yoga, exercise, and vitamins. You disconnect from all the things causing you physical or emotional trauma. If you do not change, you may not survive to the next and last stage of our life cycle. In other words, you take responsibility for (become the bearer of) the waters of your own life.

The symbol for Aquarius is a man pouring water out of a pitcher. It is the perfect illustration of man as the bearer of the waters of his own life. If you do not change your ways, you are literally pouring the waters of your own life out onto the ground. In folklore, this stage is considered an age of enlightenment, and as you will see for yourselves, it signifies an age of enlightenment for the entire human race, as well.

An interesting thing happens when sunlight shines through falling water droplets...you get a rainbow, like a bridge over troubled waters. Just saying. More on that later. When you take responsibility for (become the bearer of) the waters of your own life you become AQUARIUS, THE WATER BEARER.

CAPRICORNUS, THE SEA-GOAT

(age ~??; senior citizen/death/rebirth?)

Capricornus

Now having the wisdom of living a full life, we return to the Capricornus stage, the intelligent creatures that can excellently navigate the waters of life. Remember, all progress in life is like a spiral ramp. As senior citizens, most have learned to navigate their way around this thing we call life. They have learned from experience and spend their "golden" years doing only as they please, hopefully.

If you ever saw your grandparents, retired, enjoying life with frequent cruises or vacations, avoiding drama and conflict, spoiling their grandkids, and avoiding traffic and crowds and saving money by attending an early bird special dinner so as to be home and snug as a bug in a rug before dark, you are witnessing, first hand, intelligent creatures that have learned to excellently navigate the waters of life!

This is the last stage of our life cycle. After a full life, we enjoy our golden years as intelligent creatures who can excellently navigate the waters of life. According to the zodiac, after life has ended, we are to take that magical journey (from life to death) and then are reborn as CAPRICORNUS, THE SEA GOAT, and the cycle begins anew.

The zodiac does tell us, in pictograph form, the story of the human life cycle. We will all go through all of these stages in our own lives, whether we actually get married, have kids or not, just as the ancients who created the zodiac did, and just as all future generations will do. The zodiac truly is the revered circle of life!

Of significance is that the zodiac pictograph applies to all people. Every mammal ever born was the "Sea-Goat" (Capricornus).

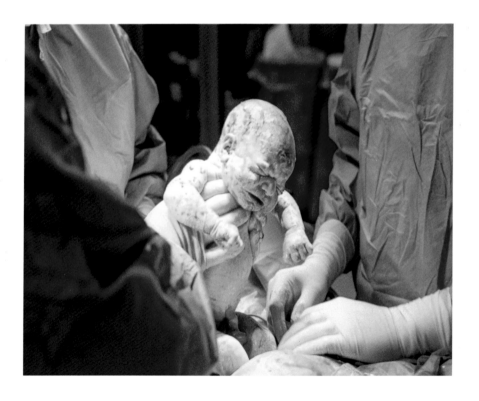

Every crawling, teething infant spent time as the "Hunter" (Sagittarius).

Every walking, talking toddler was the "Serpent Bearer" (Ophiuchus).

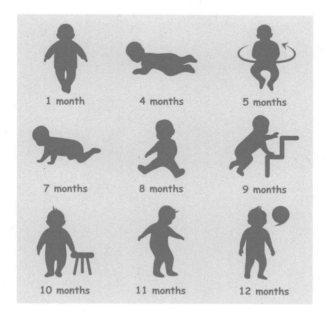

Every child entering the terrible twos started acting like the "Scorpion" (Scorpius).

Every measuring/counting child entered the "Scales" phase (Libra).

Every child who started school, the beginning of their social life, took their turn at being the "Maiden" (Virgo).

Every child who let their hair grow out while enjoying the start of youth activities with their "pack" of friends was the "Lion" (Leo).

Every child entering their teenage years has to beware the dangers lurking in the waters of life…the "Crab" (Cancer).

All persons who ever wed or merged with another to form their own family were the Lovers (Gemini).

New parents all go through the rules and discipline phase as the "Bull" (Taurus).

Preparing the baby for sleep

Parents who set up a rules and reward system for their toddlers, with a degree of negotiation, become the "Ram" (Aries).

Parents, raising their family in a community of similarly situated families, become the "Fish" (Pisces).

Every person who hits mid-life and changes their lifestyle for the better becomes the "Water Bearer" (Aquarius).

Every person who lives long enough to be a senior citizen, once again becomes the "Sea Goat" (Capricornus).

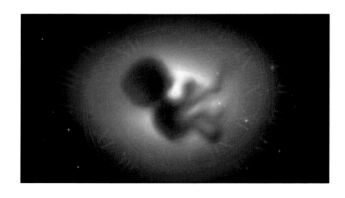

PART TWO

AS ABOVE, SO BELOW

The zodiac is indeed the revered and exalted "circle of life." However, the story does not stop there. If the zodiac tells the life cycle stages of one single human being, it must also tell us the story of the development of the entire human race in the same or parallel stages. This is known as the principle of "as above, so below." Whatever happens on the small scale, also happens on the large scale, and vice-versa. This is a philosophical maxim that is found everywhere in nature and in manmade systems. Almost all of our major religions have some prayer or reference to "on Earth as it is in heaven" or some similar statement. It is a philosophical maxim that we have understood for ages. The principal of "as above, so below" is considered the first law of the universe and has been associated with the zodiac ever since the zodiac was first created.

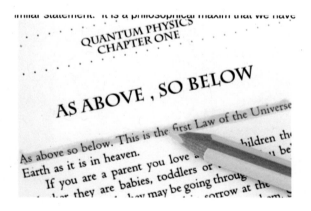

An example of as above, so below is found in the gestation of one human baby in its mother's womb. The gestation of one human baby replays the entirety of evolution from single celled organisms all the way up to human beings. All of human evolution is replayed in the gestation of one human baby. Another example is a public utility grid. The grid of a single block is a microcosm of the utility grid for the entire neighborhood, which is a microcosm of the entire district, which is a microcosm of the entire township, which is a microcosm of the utility grid of the entire county, and so on.

There are countless examples of "as above, so below" throughout nature and manmade systems. It tells us that the micro and the macro must develop along the same patterns. Ancient writings tell us that the principle of "as above, so below" applies to the zodiac. Therefore, if we apply the principal of "as above, so below" to the zodiac we should see the life cycle stages of one human as a microcosm of the life cycle stages of the entire human race. If the zodiac is the life cycle story of one human, it must, by definition, tell the life cycle story of the entire human civilization (as seen through the eyes of those living in Mesopotamia thousands of years ago). It <u>must</u> happen this way! It cannot develop in any other pattern! This is what "as above, so below" means!

This is where the zodiac's true predictive power comes in. Since the life cycle of the entire human race will mirror that of an individual, the entire human civilization will evolve in the same or similar steps as the individual. This allows us to predict the stages in the development of human civilization in the future. More importantly, we can also use the zodiac to see where we as a people came from and what happened in what order in the development of modern human civilization. As you will see, the zodiac is the history of humanity written in the stars, as seen by those living in Mesopotamia thousands of years ago. I repeat that. The zodiac is the history (and future) of humanity written in the stars!

In order to understand how the zodiac is the history (and future) of humanity written in the stars, a brief explanation of the ages and how those ages describe our history and future is in order.

From tracking the movement of the stars over thousands of years, ancient star gazers noticed that although the sun goes through all of the zodiac constellations, in a counterclockwise circle, in familiar order, every year, the sun is just shy of making a complete circle each year. It happens slowly, but it appears that our sun is moving backwards or clockwise through the constellations when measured at the same time every year. Please note that going backwards or "clockwise" through the constellations is the same way we measured the stages of one individual human life.

The Greek astronomer, Hipparchus, is credited with calculating that the sun moves easterly/backwards/clockwise through the constellations at the rate of one degree every 72 years. The sun therefore moves through one-twelfth of the circle (a new constellation) approximately every 2,160 years. It takes almost 26,000 years for the sun to make a complete loop clockwise through all the zodiac constellations. This is known as the "Great Year," as coined by Plato.

[Side note: It would have taken many lifetimes to calculate a one degree movement of the sun every 72 years, perhaps hundreds or thousands of years of study.]

The sun's apparent movement backwards through the constellations is called the "precession of the equinoxes." We call it a precession because the sun appears to be slowly going backwards/preceding/clockwise through the constellations. We measure this clockwise movement on the same day each year (the equinox) and draw our calculations from there. The day of the year that we use to make these comparative measurements is the Vernal (spring) Equinox, which is roughly March 21, each year. The reason we use the Equinox as a measuring point is two-fold. First, the Equinoxes (spring and fall) are the only two times each year when the Earth's equator is parallel with the ecliptic plane that the sun appears to travel on. We have equal day and equal night …equinox. The ring of stars of the zodiac appear to encircle our equator on only the two equinoxes each year.

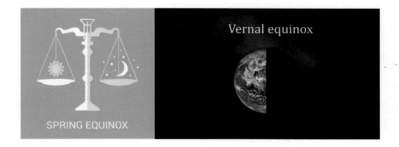

We use the Vernal (spring) equinox as a measuring point because the Spring Equinox was considered to be the beginning of the astronomical year. It was considered to be the beginning of the astronomical year because following the Spring Equinox the days became longer than the night. Light conquers darkness and all the plants would soon thereafter bloom and all the spring newborns followed. It is why we call baby mammals "offspring." Humans have been celebrating the Spring Equinox since antiquity.

Remember, the sun is always in front of one of the constellations of the zodiac, at all times. The word "Age" refers to what constellation the sun is in front of when it rises on the Vernal (Spring) Equinox (March 21). You cannot actually see the constellation when the sun is in front of it, but we know where the sun is relative to the other constellations. (You can now use a cell phone app to see exactly where the sun is relative to the zodiac constellations behind it at all times.)

When the modern zodiac was formalized, we were in the Age of Aries, which means that the sun was in the "house" of, or in front of the constellation Aries when it rose on the Vernal (Spring) Equinox. For the last 2,000 years or so, the sun has been in the constellation Pisces on the Spring Equinox, so we are deemed to be in the "Age of Pisces." Soon, the sun will be in front of the constellation Aquarius on the Spring Equinox, and we will be considered to be in the Age of Aquarius. More on the Age of Aquarius later.

[Interesting side note: The modern astrological zodiac (astrology) was formalized during the Age of Aries the Ram by the Babylonians. They made all of their measurements based upon where the sun, planets, and stars were positioned at that time (the sun was in front of Aries on the Spring Equinox when they made their measurements). This is why Aries appears first in the horoscopes.]

Now that we each know what an Age is, we can apply the maxim of "as above, so below." Using this maxim, we can match the "stages of life" to developmental steps (ages) in the evolution of human civilization. According to the maxim of "as above, so below," the stages in the development of human civilization must match or parallel the stages in the life of an individual, stage for stage, exactly, in order. Just as with the life cycle of the individual, we will measure the developments in human civilization in stages or ages. We measured the "stages" of the individual in "years of life." With respect to the entire human race, we will measure in "ages," with each age lasting approximately 2,160 years. As you will soon see for yourselves, the stages and ages do parallel each other, stage for stage.

We can only document human civilization with any degree of accuracy for the last several ages, going back to the Age of Taurus the Bull (~4,400 BCE). From the Age of Taurus the Bull, through the Age of Aries the Ram, and into the present Age (Pisces), we have archeological evidence and written language to use to document our civilization's history. We have little archeological evidence of our existence prior to the Age of Gemini (~6,600 BCE). As you will see, catastrophic events in the two prior ages, Leo the Lion (the sun roared like a lion) and Cancer the Crab (beware the dangers of the waters), erased nearly all archeological evidence of human civilization prior to that time in that area of the world. In addition, humankind barely left a carbon footprint back then.

The lack of archeological evidence beyond a certain point however, does not mean that human civilization did not exist, it is just that we are lacking definitive proofs. We know through anthropology that humans existed for hundreds of thousands of years. We are social beings. Of course we had social structure that dates farther back in history than we can document. We can, however, use the zodiac and the template of the life cycle of an individual to fill in the missing archeological evidence, or better yet, simply connect the dots!

We were all taught that the Sumerian culture was the first recognized modern human civilization. Recent archeological finds, however, are proving that human civilization does, in fact, go back much further than originally believed. One example is the is the discovery of the Aratta civilization, which lived in caves in what is present day Ukraine. This site dates back some 24,000 years, to approximately 22,000 BCE, which was, up until recently, thought impossible. This site shows that the Aratta peoples had knowledge of the stars, religion, primitive language, and social structure. We now know that there was sophisticated human civilization as far back at 22,000 BCE. This discovery is re-rewriting our understanding of modern human history, and as you will see, this discovery fits perfectly into the zodiac timeline.

Another recent archeological find is the discovery of Gobekli Tepe, a large stone-carved worship complex in Northern Turkey, which dates back over 12,000 years to around 10,000 BCE. This site shows not only evidence of pilgrimage from long distances, it also shows a sophisticated knowledge of astronomy, agriculture, masonry, artistry, engineering and religion. This means that mankind already had a sophisticated social dynamic, with specialized division of labor, at least as far back as 10,000 BCE, thousands of years older than conventional wisdom would have us believe.

Discoveries in climatology and geology also reveal significant changes in the climate and living environment for humans that coincide with the changes in the Ages. For example, there is evidence that the worst part of the Ice Age came to an abrupt end around 22,000 BCE with catastrophic flooding thereafter which decimated much of the world's low-lying flora and fauna. The Aratta civilization survived the ice age and flooding, by living in caves in the hills and mountains. This occurred at the beginning of the Age of Capricornus (the intelligent creatures that can navigate/survive the waters of life).

There is evidence of either comet fragment impacts or some sort of solar related impacts hit the northern hemisphere of Earth around 10,800 BCE, which decimated much of the northern hemisphere's flora and fauna, such as saber-toothed tigers and woolly mammoths, and then plunged the Earth into a mini ice age known as the Younger Dryas. Thereafter the planet's temperature rose rapidly, significantly warming the planet, slowly causing sea levels to rise by hundreds of feet. This occurred during the Age of Leo the Lion. The lion's mane is symbolic of the sun's corona. This symbol tells us that during the Age of Leo, the sun roared like a lion. And, there is evidence of catastrophic flooding in the Age of Cancer the Crab (beware the dangers of the waters of life) around 7,700 BCE, which is the basis for our epic flood stories.

There are also substantial advances in human civilization associated with the change in Ages. For example, Hinduism arose during the Age of Taurus the Bull. This religion contains much bull symbolism, and cows are still considered sacred to this very day. At the same time Hinduism was rising in the East, the Middle East saw the development of enforced religious practices, such as sacrifice of the first born, in the Age of Taurus the Bull. Enforced religious practices and bull symbolism were replaced by voluntary, monotheistic religious practices and ram symbolism at the beginning of the Age of Aries the Ram, which was followed by new monotheistic religions, and fish symbolism, at the beginning of the Age of Pisces.

Just as with the story of the individual, the story of the birth of modern human civilization must start with the Age of Capricornus, the symbol for birth, death, and rebirth (as above, so below). So, I wrote down the Ages and approximate starting dates in a list going backwards from modern times all the way back to the Age of Capricornus (~21,700 BCE). I allotted approximately 2,160 years for each Age but rounded things off to make it simpler to follow.

I then listed the description of things that happened in each Age next to the zodiac symbols, and lo and behold, they match exactly, if and only if, we start with the Age of Capricornus. I then matched that list to the life cycle stages of the individual to see if I can find three stages and ages in a row that match. Remember, we must find one-sixth of the circle that matches exactly. If we find that, we can then define the entire circle.

As discussed above, we only have three ages of written human history (Taurus, Aries, and Pisces), so I focused my attention on them to see if I can find any matches. As you can guess, I immediately saw a match. The Age of Taurus the Bull saw "enforced religious practices." We know this from the Bible and the story of Abraham. At the time of Abraham, there was an enforced religious practice requiring parents to sacrifice their first born. Abraham is noted for refusing to follow such religious mandate, setting up a new relationship with God. The Age of Taurus the Bull matches the new parent phase of life. Both the Taurus stage of an individual's life and the Age of Taurus the Bull have "enforced practices" with strict adherence to the rules/laws.

Next, I saw that the Age of Aries brought a new religion and understanding of God. God was not like a bull who might harm you, God was more like a ram, protecting and guiding his flock. Two new concepts arose when discussing God. The first is that if you follow God's laws, he will protect you (like any ram would protect his flock). The second is the act of negotiating with God. One could now ask God for forgiveness, protections, and/or blessings. This matches the Aries the Ram phase of an individual's life. Both stages have the elements of "follow the rules and be rewarded" and "negotiating," (just like a ram must negotiate his way up a steep cliff face). We now have two stages and Ages that match. We need one more.

The next age is Pisces, the age we have been living in for the last 2,000 years or so. This age started around the same time that Christianity started. Fish symbolism is associated with Christianity. In this Age, we have conquered the planet, filling every niche of society and the habitable areas of the globe. We as a human civilization have spent the Age of Pisces doing what humans do, just as a family does what families do during the Pisces stage of their lives. Again, both stage and Age match.

I now saw three ages that match the stages of life, in order. I remained skeptical and decided to check one more stage, and that is the upcoming Age of Aquarius. For the individual, Aquarius is middle age where we change our ways and start taking care of our bodies. I immediately noted that we humans have, over the last 50 years, started to worry and care for Mother Earth, the body we all live on. We have started conservation efforts and enacted clean water and clean air acts. We have started recycling and using renewable sources of energy. We are starting to take care of this body (Mother Earth), so we as a human race are acting as if we are hitting middle age.

I was now convinced that there is an undeniable pattern. The life cycle of the entire human race does indeed follow the stages of life of an individual, stage for stage. I could now write down a chart matching the Ages to stages of life, and lo and behold, it re-writes our history and puts everything in its time ordered place. As you will see, the zodiac only confirms what we already knew had happened in our history. It just puts things on a new timeline. As you see, the zodiac truly is the history of human civilization written in the stars!

Below is written a time-line description of the evolution of human civilization as told through the zodiac symbols (as seen through the eyes of the peoples living in Mesopotamia thousands of years ago). It is important to keep in mind that all growth and development is gradual, like a spiral ramp, and things transition slowly over time. However, it is easier to measure in steps, stages, or ages. The development of the entire human civilization is measured in ages; however, remember, this is a spiral ramp so things are always slowly transitioning with giant leaps every so often. Things always overlap and each new age or stage is an add-on to the elements of the prior ages/stages.

Please take a look at the chart, below. As you will see, human civilization starts in its infancy and then follows the same stages, in the same order as the stages in the life of one individual (apex predator/hunter, development of language, development of trade and commerce/ measuring, etc.), Please note that the story of the evolution of human civilization matches or parallels the life cycle of the individual, stage for stage, only if we start with the Age of Capricornus.

The older ages, for which there is little, if any, archeological evidence, are drawn from the template of the individual and applied to the limited archeological, geological and climatological information available at this time. As you will see, the zodiac only confirms what happened, in what order, and provides a time-table for each stage. Approximate starting dates for each age have been added for frame of reference purposes only, not for technical accuracy. Remember, the story is supposed to be illustrative, not necessarily technically accurate as to dates. Remember, a lot of this story is from pre-history, carried on by oral tradition for thousands of years before it was written down!

Zodiac = The Story of Us

Zodiac Symbol	Age	Stage of Life
Capricornus (the sea goat)	0	Birth/Rebirth Newborn
Sagittarius (the hunter)	1	Crawling, teething infant
Ophiuchus (the serpent bearer)	1	Toddler (masters language)
Scorpius (the scorpion)	2	Terrible Twos striking out at parents
Libra (the scales)	3	Measuring/Counting Child
Virgo (the maiden)	5	Introduction to society (school)
Leo (the lion)	8	Begin social activities (let hair down)
Cancer (the crab)	13	Teenager Beware the dangers in the waters of life
Gemini (the lovers/twins)	21	Marriage/Merging new household
Taurus (the bull)	21+	Having infant children (enforced practices)
Aries (the ram)	21++	Parents of toddlers (follow the rules) negotiation
Pisces (the fish)	21+++	Family doing as they do (school of fish)
Aquarius (the water bearer)	midlife	Middle age Bearer of the waters of one's life
Capricornus (the seat goat)	Senior Citizen	Senior citizen death and rebirth navigate waters of life

Zodiac = The Story of Us

Stage of Human Development	apprx Year	Zodiac Age
Birth/Rebirth of Civilization	21,700 BCE	Capricornus (the sea goat)
Apex Predator hunter	19,500	Sagittarius (the hunter)
Masters Language and surroundings	19,000	Ophiuchus (the serpent bearer)
Drying up (desert) warring/striking out	17,300	Scorpius (the scorpion)
Beginning of Commerce/ Trade and accounting	15,100	Libra (the scales)
Introduction of society/ social structure	12,800	Virgo (the maiden)
Sun Roared like a lion (solar impacts)	10,800	Leo (the lion)
cities under water epic flood stories beware the dangers	8600	Cancer (the crab)
Merging of people's to form modern society	6500	Gemini (the lovers/twins)
Enforced religious practices	4400	Taurus (the bull)
Monotheism Follow the rules negociate with God	2200	Aries (the ram)
Humans doing as they do Brotherhood of mankind	~48 BCE	Pisces (the fish)
Middle age take care of Earth bear the waters of life	~2112	Aquarius (the water bearer)
Navigate the waters of life space colonization? mankind evolves?	4300	Capricornus (the seat goat)

Come along with me as we together rediscover the true story of us!

THE AGE OF CAPRICORNUS, THE SEA GOAT

(~21,700 BCE)

Capricorn

Capricornus is the intelligent beast that can navigate/survive the waters of life. The climatological records reveal that around 22,000 BCE the harshest part of the Ice Age came to an abrupt end. For whatever reason, there was an instant and rapid, substantial warming of the planet. The global temperature rose something like four degrees in a short period of time. Ice that had covered much of the land masses began to melt rapidly, causing worldwide, catastrophic flooding to occur. Much of the low-lying flora and fauna were decimated and/or forced to relocate to the hills and mountains to survive.

Modern humans managed to survive the worst part of the Ice Age and subsequent flooding by living in caves underground up in the hills and mountains, working together in groups, and using their superior mammalian intelligence. As the weather improved mankind emerged from their cave cities and began to spread out and interact with other groups, clans, and/or tribes. This was the infancy of human civilization. The Aratta Civilization is proof of this. The archeological evidence found in caves in Ukraine shows that mankind (the Aratta civilization) survived the worst part of the Ice Age and subsequent flooding by living in caves in the hills and mountains. Archeological evidence also shows that they had a definitive, advanced social structure as far back as 21,700 BCE, which would be the beginning of the Age of Capricornus.

It appears from the cave artwork that they not only had social structure, but they had a primitive language. They had religion, laws, and a social dynamic. They even had agreements with other nearby groups for mutual protection. Their cave artwork also shows that their gods were the forerunners of the Sumerian gods and Sumerian culture itself. Sumerian clay tablets say their forerunners were taught by the "Annunaki," which means "those who from above the clouds came." These same clay tablets indicate that those who "from above the clouds came" are the same peoples who purportedly taught math and astronomy to the Sumerians. We still use the 60- and 10-digit mathematics purportedly taught by the Annunaki to the Sumerians. Perhaps the Aratta civilization and the Annunaki and Sumerians are all one and the same peoples or are somehow closely related in lineage. I leave it to the archeologists to explore the connection.

As the Anunnaki supposedly taught math and astronomy to the Sumerians, it is extremely likely, although highly speculative, that the Aratta/Anunnaki may have also taught the zodiac to the Sumerians. Only time will tell if we can prove that link.

When you think of the birth/infancy of human civilization, think of the intelligent creatures that navigated (survived) the waters of life, CAPRICORNUS, THE SEA GOAT.

[Please note that this stage of human development parallels the "newborn" stage of the individual human. Both had to successfully navigate the waters of life. Both are a beginning. The character of a half goat, half fish "intelligent creature that can successfully navigate the waters of life" applies to both the individual newborn and the newborn human civilization.]

THE AGE OF SAGITTARIUS, THE HUNTER

(~19,500 BCE)

Around this time, mankind became the apex predator/hunter, perhaps due in part to the decimation in the prior age of many species that preyed upon man. Mankind was now living above ground and conquering its immediate environment. Hunting required the use of primitive weapons and coordinated and cooperative hunting strategies, and the sharing of spoils. At some point in the evolution of human civilization, humans became the apex predator. The zodiac tells us it happened in this age. When you think of mankind as apex predator/hunter, think of SAGITTARIUS, THE HUNTER.

[Please note that this stage matches the "hunter" phase of a crawling, teething infant's life. Both are hunters practicing their primeval skills. The character of a half human, half horse, holding a bow and arrow is the perfect example of baby humans (and all baby mammals) and early human civilization going through the "hunter" phase.]

THE AGE OF OPHIUCHUS, THE SERPENT BEARER

(~19,000 BCE)

Ophiuchus

Although this stage is not included in the 12 "signs" of the zodiac, this stage is a distinctly separate evolutionary stage for human civilization, hence its appearance in the zodiac. As with the Fibonacci progression and given its place in the zodiac wheel, this age started shortly after mankind became apex predator.

It is theorized that the development of our language was closely associated with the need to communicate when hunting. Therefore, shortly after mankind became the "hunter," we developed language or perhaps perfected it such that we could then communicate with others outside our immediate tribe or group. Remember, the symbol of a snake has often been used in ancient art to represent the tongue and objects of desire.

We can also theorize, by comparing this Age to the Ophiuchus stage of an individual's life (mastering language and its immediate environment) that mankind began to master nature and domesticate animals in this age. For example, we may have begun to dig wells to draw water and cisterns to store water and started basic nomadic agriculture, increasing man's dominance over nature and the creatures within our domain.

It is also theorized that humankind began to domesticate dogs and other animals at this time. We used dogs to hunt and herd animals, like reindeer and wild cattle, goats and sheep. Domesticated dogs also provided protection for mankind and the flocks and herds mankind fed from. Recent archeological discoveries and cave paintings indicate that man may have also started domesticating beasts of burden and birds of prey during this age.

At some point in the development of human civilization, we had to develop language and master our immediate environments. According to the zodiac and the life cycle of an individual, humankind accomplished this in the Age of OPHIUCHUS, THE SERPENT BEARER.

[Please note that this stage parallels the walking, talking toddler who has mastered its tongue and the objects within its control. The zodiac character of a man holding a snake applies to both the individual, standing, talking, and grasping objects of its desire, and human civilization learning to control animals, its immediate environment and its tongue (language).]

THE AGE OF SCORPIUS, THE SCORPION

(~17,300 BCE)

Scorpio

The zodiac tells us that during this age, many places in the then known world surrounding the Fertile Crescent became arid. Places that were once fertile became desert, and river beds dried up, causing most people in Mesopotamia (and possibly Ukraine) to move to the Fertile Crescent and other freshwater-rich places to survive. We still use the word "deserted" today to describe something that was once fertile but is now desolate. (The Sumerian clay tablets say that their forerunners moved to Mesopotamia from their original homeland after it became arid. May have happened at this time?)

Condensing of populations into a smaller living areas and dwindling resources were grounds for hostilities over territories, resources, and especially fresh water. When you think of fertile places on Earth turning to desert and mankind's struggles and fighting over territories. resources, and water, think of the desert, think of a scorpion…. SCORPIUS, THE SCORPION.

[Please note that this Age parallels the terrible twos stage, where the child pulls away from its parents unconditional love to form its own identity with sharp, stinging words. The zodiac character of a scorpion applies to both the toddler striking out and humankind striking out/warring over water, and the scorpion is also symbolic of the desert.]

THE AGE OF LIBRA, THE SCALES

(~15,100 BCE)

Libra

As a result of humans congregating and living together in larger communities, becoming more and more sedentary, mankind began to trade among themselves, their neighbors, and with other communities. Commerce, trade, and accounting started in this Age. At some point in the development of human civilization, we began commerce, trade, and accounting. Although we have no conclusive archeological evidence of this, the zodiac tells us that it happened at this time. When you think of the beginning of commerce, trade, and accounting, think LIBRA, THE SCALES.

[Please note that this stage parallels the measuring, counting stage of the three-year-old. In both instances, there is counting and measuring going on. What better way to represent both than by use of scales?]

THE AGE OF VIRGO, THE VIRGIN/MAIDEN

(~12,800 BCE)

Virgo

At this time, humankind, living together in ever larger, sedentary groups, created its first large-scale societies. There was now large-scale social structure. These primitive first societies saw specialized labor and the hierarchy of social status and structure. This was the foundation of our modern social structure where many people live together in cooperation, in different classes and status, operating as a unified "whole," with all citizens working together for the common good, each with their own specified place in society.

Large-scale societies, which later grew into our oldest cities, started in this Age. We have scant archeological evidence from this time period; however, the zodiac tells us society was introduced at this time. In addition, think of the logic. Before we had cities, we had people living together in large communities where social status and social structure first formed. This had to start long before our first cities were ever built.

When you think of the introduction of society, think VIRGO, THE VIRGIN/MAIDEN.

[Please note that this stage parallels the individual being introduced to society at or around age five. In both instances, we have the introduction of society, brand new, fresh and innocent. What better way to represent newness than the symbol of a maiden/virgin who by definition is brand new, fresh, and innocent?]

THE AGE OF LEO, THE LION

(~10,800 BCE)

Leo

The lion's mane often represents the corona of the sun in ancient art. In this age, the sun roared like a lion. Recent scientific finds tell us that comet fragments, a solar flare, or some other solar event hit the northern hemisphere around 10,800 BCE, right at the beginning of the Age of Leo the Lion. There are millions of animals who died instantly at this time and were frozen in the permafrost of Siberia with food still in their mouths, as well as geological evidence of this event. This event caused a mini ice age known as the "Younger Dryas," which may have been caused by the sun's rays being blocked out due to dust, etc., in the atmosphere.

The solar impacts and subsequent freeze decimated much of the northern hemisphere's flora and fauna, such as wooly mammoths and saber-toothed tigers. It also caused mankind to once again go live underground. There is archeological evidence of cave cities in Turkey that date back to this Age. We now know why. Something happened that severely disrupted life on Earth (particularly in the northern hemisphere) at this time.

[Side note: The story of "Sodom & Gomorrah" probably originated from events that happened during this age. Remember, both cities were destroyed by fiery objects hailing down from the skies. The Bible tells us that the event was so devastating, it turned Lott's wife into a pillar of salt. (It means that those cities were not destroyed by God because the people were wicked.) The cities were unfortunately hit by comet fragments or some other solar event. This also means that we had cities as far back as this age.]

According to the zodiac, the sun roared like a lion at this time, and we now have the geological and archeological evidence to prove it. Mankind went back to living underground for hundreds of years in that area of the world. In addition, ancient Vedic writings tell of an ancient event where the sky lit up with the brightness of a thousand suns. Although those living in India at the time were probably protected from the worst part of the calamity due to the Himalaya Mountains, it is clear that something catastrophic happened in the northern hemisphere and the zodiac (and geological and archeological evidence) tells us that it happened in this age.

Following this solar event, the Earth plunged into a mini ice age called the Younger Dryas, which lasted several hundred years. Thereafter, the climate got substantially warmer. The polar caps had been melting rapidly, causing sea levels to slowly rise, globally, by hundreds of feet, eventually leaving older cities and structures on the coasts permanently under water. We see evidence of these cities and structures all over the globe. We now know that these structures and coastal cities started to go permanently under water when the ocean levels rose. We know from geology and the zodiac that this happened slowly and as a direct result of the sun roaring like a lion in this age.

We can theorize that our first sun-worship religions started after humankind was hurt by the sun (or pieces of the sun falling to Earth). Despite the devastation, mankind eventually began to flourish in the new climate. Man's first large scale worship and stone celebratory sites were constructed during this Age, perhaps in thanks for having survived the global disaster. Gobekli Tepe, an ancient worship complex in northern Turkey, constructed in elaborate, carved pillars of stone, was built around 10,000 BCE. This site shows evidence of pilgrimage from long distances, and a complex knowledge of agriculture, astronomy, masonry, engineering, and religion. It means that mankind had a complex social dynamic, with specialized division of labor, as far back as the Age of Leo.

[Side note: The Sphynx, is theorized to originally have had a proportionally sized lion's head. It would have been facing the Constellation Leo the Lion on the Spring Equinox, if and only if, it was built during the Age of Leo. The body of the Sphynx has water erosion marks that took thousands of years to form, where the now disproportionately smaller head, carved into the likeness a pharaoh, has no water erosion marks. It stopped raining in that area of the world around 7,000 BCE. This is proof that the Sphynx was originally built with a lion's head in the Age of Leo, long before it stopped raining in that area. The decayed lion's head was modified later on, when the pyramids were built and the temple restored.]

When you think of the sun roaring like a lion, think of LEO, THE LION.

[Please note that this stage parallels the beginning of social activities stage of a child's life. For the child, it lets its hair grow out and travels in a pack of friends. For human society, the sun roared like a lion. What better symbol captures both stages as the lion's mane both represents "letting your hair grow out" and the sun roaring like a lion?]

THE AGE OF CANCER, THE CRAB

(~8,600 BCE)

Cancer

There is evidence of the second solar event around 9,600 BCE and one or more catastrophic flooding events thereafter. The sea levels that had been slowly rising since the Age of Leo the Lion, by then, resulted in many coastal cities, temples, and structures being left permanently underwater. Such evidence is found all around the world. Cultures from all over the world have historic tales of catastrophic flooding (which may or may not be related).

One such flooding event occurred around 7,700 BCE during the Age of Cancer the Crab (beware the dangers of the waters of life). The Mediterranean Sea, which had been slowly rising since the Age of Leo the Lion, filled to the breaking point and in a catastrophic event, poured through the Bosphorus Straits and into the freshwater Black Lake, turning it into the much larger, saltwater Black Sea we know today. Multitudes died instantly, fertile land went permanently under water, and civilization in Mesopotamia was decimated for centuries to come. A major food and freshwater source was turned permanently into undrinkable salt water. (This cataclysmic event is probably the basis of our epic flood stories that emanate out of the Middle East, "Noah" and the "Epic of Gilgamesh". It also means, however, that the flood was not God punishing mankind. It was an unfortunate natural disaster caused by comet impacts in the prior age).

Not only was there catastrophic flooding, wells and cisterns got contaminated; insects, swamps, swamp creatures, and water borne diseases ravaged mankind in that area of the world for generation after generation. In fact, this age was so deadly for mankind in that area of the world that our most horrible disease (cancer) is named after it (same root word).

If you ever unknowingly stepped on a crab while barefoot at the shoreline, you will know all too well to beware the dangers lurking in the waters of life, CANCER, THE CRAB.

[Please note that this stage parallels the beginning of the teenage years in a child's development. In both instances, we are cautioned to beware the dangers lurking in the waters of life. For the individual, they must be wary of the dangers lurking in the waters of life when first discovering the outside world for themselves. For human civilization, we literally had to suffer and beware the dangers of the waters. What better way to represent this notion than a crab, who poses danger to anyone walking barefoot in murky waters.]

THE AGE OF GEMINI, THE LOVERS/TWINS

(~6,600 BCE)

Gemini

After civilization in the Middle East was once again devastated in the Age of Cancer, it began to rebuild itself. Our oldest large-scale civilizations arose during this age. The earliest known cuneiform clay tablets containing our written histories and religious doctrines can also be traced back to this age. We have archeological evidence of the forerunners of the Sumerian Empire rising at this time, and until recently, we thought that this was the beginning of human civilization. We now know that human civilization goes back much further in time than this age. The Age of Gemini was not the beginning of civilization, but was the rebuilding of civilization after two ages of catastrophic events. This explains why, when our first cities were just built in this age, we already had currency, agriculture, markets, politics, social structure, etc. It would have taken hundreds and probably thousands of years for these things to develop.

The Gemini lovers, sometimes referred to as the Gemini "Twins," represent the duality of man, the old and the new, the sophisticated and unsophisticated man, the people of different sub-cultures, coming together, merging, to form modern society. The concepts of good and evil and the dualistic nature of things (light/dark, tall/short) were developed during this age. When you think of the duality of man, and a merging of peoples to form our modern civilization, think GEMINI, THE LOVERS/TWINS.

[Please note that this stage parallels the marriage stage of life. There is a merging to make a new whole. The symbol of lovers/twins is the perfect representation of this merging. In the individual's case, this merging is followed by creating a new home and family of their own, with its own identity. In the case of human civilization, it represents the duality of man coming together to form modern civilization.]

THE AGE OF TAURUS, THE BULL

(~4,400 BCE)

Taurus

In the East, the Age of Taurus the Bull saw the rise of Hinduism, which is rich in bull symbolism and bull worship. Cows were deemed sacred to Hindus, and are still considered sacred to this very day.

While India saw the rise of Hinduism, Mesopotamia saw the rise of enforced polytheistic religious practices. Following the devastating flooding in that area of the world in the prior Age of Cancer the Crab, it was believed that everyone needed to toe-the-line when it came to God so God would not try to wipe us out again. Remember, most people in that area of the world thought the prior catastrophic flooding was God's attempt to wipe humanity from the planet for being prideful and wicked. God or "the gods" were seen as having the temperament of a bull. You have to watch your step around a bull and always be on your guard or else the bull might harm you (or throw a flood at you). Bull symbolism, bull artwork, and bull worship appeared in Mesopotamia, and as far West as Crete (think of the Minotaur) during the Age of Taurus the Bull.

During this Age, all people were required to perform certain religious rituals. If you did not go along with the rest of the masses, you could be made an example of because people were afraid of offending God or the gods. We know from the Biblical story of Abraham that during the Age of Taurus the Bull, people were expected to sacrifice their first born. Abraham, who symbolizes the upcoming new Age of Aries, defies this, and as the Bible tells us, he was thereafter forced to move himself and his extended family to the other side of the river to escape retribution from his neighbors who were fearful that God would punish them for Abraham violating the religious mandates of the time.

We still use the terms, "Stubborn as a bull," and, "You mess with the bull, you get the horns," and police officers still use a "bull horn" to speak to the masses. Enforced, religious observance in Mesopotamia is the theme here.

When you think of forced religious observance and strict, enforced adherence to religious law, think TAURUS, THE BULL.

[Please note that this stage parallels the "new parent" phase of an individual's life. There is a required need for strict adherence to rules, schedules and practices. What better symbol than a stubborn, inflexible bull?]

THE AGE OF ARIES, THE RAM

(~2,200 BCE)

Aries

During this Age, some people began to challenge the forced, polytheistic, religious observance policies. Abraham, the symbol of the Age of Aries the Ram, is touted in religious doctrines to be the first in Western society to refuse to follow the local, mandatory practice of sacrificing the first born. This set up a new relationship with God. Following that event, Abraham had to move his family to the other side of the river to prevent retaliation from his neighbors, who were fearful that God would punish them for Abraham's refusal to follow the religious mandates of the time.

[Side note: The word Abraham is actually a mix of middle-eastern dialect with Sanskrit. "A" in the middle east denotes "son of" and "Braham" is one of many ways of pronouncing "Brahma," which in Sanskrit means "God," so "Abraham" actually means "son of god", not "father of many"…although he certainly was.]

Certain people came to see God, not with the temperament of a stubborn bull, but more like a ram. If you follow God's laws and act like a good flock member, God, like a ram, will protect you, as any ram would protect his flock. You could have a personal relationship with God, on your own terms. As long as you follow God's laws, you can observe and celebrate life as you wish. In addition, you could now negotiate with God such as ask God for forgiveness, blessings and/or protections. Ram symbolism and ram artwork became common.

It is during this time that Judaism took its present form. While others still responded to the bull horn, the Hebrews began using the ram's horn as a call to prayer. Only those who knew what the sound of the ram's horn meant answered the call. Judaism still uses the ram's horn as a call to prayer to this very day.

In addition, one of the biggest imports of the Exodus story is Moses using the laws of the Age of Aries the Ram (the 10 Commandments) to, once and for all, vanquish the enforced religious practices of the golden calf (Taurus the Bull). The Moses narrative is actually a story about the change in age from Taurus to Aries. The new age, with a new voluntary, monotheistic understanding of man's relationship with God, finally triumphed over the old, forced religious practices of the prior age. It was a giant evolutionary leap for humankind. We still celebrate Moses in the West to this very day.

When you think of the development of monotheism, and the new doctrine of "follow God's laws, and God will protect you like a ram would protect his flock," think ARIES, THE RAM.

[Please note that this stage parallels the "parent of toddlers" stage of life. In both stages a reward-based system is installed into the situation, "follow the rules and be rewarded" is a theme common to both. Negotiation is also common to both. The character of a ram representing the authority figure who protects and controls yet grants freedoms, rewards and punishments to its observant flock is a perfect example of the reward-based system. Follow God's laws and celebrate life as you will.]

THE AGE OF PISCES, THE FISH

(~48 BCE)

Pisces

In this age, a new concept developed and along with it came new monotheistic religions. The common themes were the brotherhood of humankind and that one must deny or die of the body in order to be reborn of the spirit. Fasting and water purification rituals became common. Fish is and was a fundamental icon of the Christian religion. God was now seen as being more like a loving, forgiving father figure, rather than a ram.

In order for the new age to begin, there must be a symbolic end or death of the prior age. Just like Moses symbolizes the end of Taurus the Bull and the beginning of Aries the Ram, the end of Aries the Ram must have a symbolic story associated with it. The end of Aries the Ram is symbolized by the slaughter of the "Lamb of God." Jesus' death is the symbol for the end of the Age of Aries and his symbolic resurrection represents the rise of the new Age of Pisces.

During the Age of Pisces, humanity was to learn several things: we are all fish in the same waters (brotherhood of man); the waters of life (God) are all around and inside us; and our fates are tied together (just like the fishes' tails in the constellation). It is during this Age that we humans did and still do whatever it is that humans do, when filling up and conquering a planet.

Of significance is the fact that the fish in the Constellation Pisces are looking in different directions. Those who do not see things the way you and yours do are the competition, the enemy or the infidel. 'Us vs. Them' became a common theme in the Age of Pisces. It was an important step in our evolution, allowing world conquest, economics and technology to grow and thrive. However, it was also filled with war, separation, delusion and divisiveness…to win it all at all costs, much of it in the name of God, no less.

Both ancient Greeks and Eastern Mystics called the Age of Pisces the "dark" or "iron" age, which was to be followed by a "golden age of enlightenment" (Aquarius). As you will see, they were right.

Despite all the darkness, divisiveness, and ugliness that accompanied the Age of Pisces, there have been tremendous advances in all aspects of civilization. The entire planet and every niche of society have been filled. Mankind has come to realize that there indeed is a brotherhood of all humankind, and that all of our fates are indeed tied together (like the fishes' tails in the constellation). When you think of the brotherhood of man or all of humankind as fish in the same waters, think PISCES, THE FISH.

[Please note that this stage parallels the "raising a family in a community" stage of an individual's life. The symbol of two fish representing that we are in a larger community or "school of fish," where we define everything in terms of opposites, like conservative or liberal, Us vs. Them, etc. The fish not only describes a family as part of a much larger group, living life and doing its thing, it also describes all of mankind, going through the "Us vs. Them" phase, doing its thing and coming to the realization that we are all part of a larger, global community…that we are all fish in a much larger body of water.]

THE AGE OF AQUARIUS, THE WATER BEARER

(~2012 CE)

Aquarius

This is the age that we are now entering into. The constellation is a man pouring water out of a pitcher. Humanity comes to realize that humankind is responsible for (the bearer of) the waters of all life on this planet. The melting polar caps, rising sea levels, lack of fresh drinking water, and the steaming up of the planet (all water related) are and will be the vital concern to all life on this planet in the upcoming age. If we do not change our ways, we are literally pouring the waters of life out onto the ground!

As with the life cycle of the individual, entering the Age of Aquarius means that human civilization is reaching middle age, where we must now take care of this body (Mother Earth) if we want to continue to thrive. Out of necessity, we, as a people, must and will change the way we conduct ourselves to better protect the planet and her inhabitants. For example, we are now "going green," and changing our business practices to be less harmful to the environment and are becoming more accepting of all life, even those that are different from us.

We are seeing a newfound care and respect for nature and the need to protect the animals of this planet. We are seeing demand that sentient animals be freed from captivity. Circuses and the like are on the drastic decline, as no one wants to see animals forced to live in cages and perform dangerous feats, like being forced to jump through hoops of fire. This is only one example of many.

We are not only seeing a change in the way we do things; we are witnessing a change in our offspring. Many of the younger generation are distinctly different. They are far more sensitive and compassionate. Older Pisceans call them "snowflakes" because they do not understand the new generation. The younger generation are much more sensitive and were raised to think digitally (series of numbers and symbols) where their Piscean elders were taught to think analog (map). They adapt and master the new technologies as if it was second nature to them. Did you ever see a two-year-old show their grandparents how to adjust advanced settings on their smartphones? Or watch a four-year-old play concert piano? These children are a sign of the new Age we are transitioning into. Remember, all development is like a spiral ramp, slowly transitioning. However, we can see evidence of this transition right before our very eyes, one child at a time!

When you think of mankind taking responsibility for (becoming the bearer of) the waters of life on this planet, think of AQUARIUS, THE WATER BEARER.

[Please note that this stage parallels the "midlife" stage of an individual's life. In both instances, we become the bearers of the waters of our lives. For the individual, one must now take stock of one's self and re-create themselves into a much healthier ethos, or we may not continue. For human civilization, it means that we must start taking care of our body, Mother Earth, if we want to continue thriving on this planet. We are seeing evidence of this all around us. We are going "green," recycling, conserving and protecting wildlife and domestic animals. We can see evidence of this change in our society. Humankind, as a whole, is hitting middle age. What better symbol of a human and human society as the bearers of the waters of life than a man pouring water out of a pitcher?]

THE AGE OF CAPRICORNUS, THE GOAT-FISH

(~4,100 CE)

Capricorn

The Age of Aquarius will no doubt be filled with challenges for mankind. We are going to have to significantly change the way we do things if we are to survive. I believe we will survive, come hell or high water [a clear reference to the Age of Leo (fires on Earth) and the Age of Cancer (flooding)], and that will bring us back to the Age of Capricornus...the intelligent creatures that can navigate/survive the waters of life. Remember, all growth is spiral.

Perhaps we will once again have to survive worldwide catastrophic flooding. Perhaps, humanity will evolve or create artificial life, or begin commercial space exploration, or establish colonies off the Earth, or maybe conquer disease or delay death. Perhaps we will learn to travel by way of astral projection. Perhaps we will live through some or all of these things. Any way you look at it, humanity will again be the intelligent creatures that can navigate the waters of life. When you think of humankind as intelligent creatures who can navigate the waters of life, think of CAPRICORNUS, THE SEA GOAT.

[Please note that this stage has not happened yet and will not occur for some 2,000 years from now. We can speculate from the template of the individual human being, that just as a senior citizen has learned to excellently navigate its way through this thing we call life, the entire human race will excel, expertly navigating its way through this thing we call life. We may even form a new civilization off of the Earth and start the cycle again.]

What have we learned? Conventional wisdom has led us to believe that the story of human civilization started somewhere around the Age of Gemini; however, that would mean that the story of humanity started somewhere in the middle of the human life cycle story. That cannot be. Remember, "as above, so below." If Taurus was the infancy of human civilization, it would have been designated the Sea-Goat, not the Bull. If Gemini was the infancy of human civilization, it would have been the Sea-Goat, not the Lovers. Remember, they could have drawn any picture out of any of the star groupings. They put them in a certain order, starting at a certain point, for a reason. It is not random.

The development of human civilization follows stage for stage the life cycle of one individual, if and only if, we start with the Age of Capricorn. Also, remember the individual human life cycle starts with the Capricornus. What does this mean? It means that the zodiac and the maxim of "as above, so below" tell us that humanity had its infancy in the Age of Capricornus. This means that civilization must have started around 21,700 BCE, not 6,000 or 4,000 BCE as conventional wisdom would have us believe. The stages of life and ages match, if and only if, we start with the Age of Capricornus.

Still not convinced? Think about this. Capricornus could have been placed anywhere on the zodiac circle. Anywhere! However, the creators of the zodiac chose to call the upside-down triangle of stars the Sea-Goat (newborn). They put the infancy of human civilization all the way back to when the sun was in the upside-down triangle of stars on the Spring Equinox. What does this mean, my dear readers? It means that we cannot escape the inevitable conclusion that human civilization started approximately 21,700 BCE, at least as far as the zodiac is concerned. That is why the upside-down triangle of stars is called the Sea-Goat (newborn). It means that human civilization goes all the way back to when the sun was in front of the westernmost star of the constellation Capricornus on the Spring Equinox. Like it or not! The zodiac and the maxim of "as above, so below" give us a clear road map.

The zodiac as a timeline of the life cycle of an individual human being is borne out by our current scientific understanding of human development. The human life cycle follows, almost exactly, the Fibonacci growth sequence, and we can witness these "stages of life" with our very own eyes. The human life cycle has been the same since the very beginning of humanity and will remain the same for future generations. Celebrating the stages of life is what it means to be a human on the planet Earth. This is how it goes, and if you are lucky, you will get to be every character in the zodiac story (circle of life).

Similarly, the zodiac description of the life cycle of modern human civilization follows, stage for stage, the life cycle of one individual (as above, so below). In fact, the principle of "as above, so below" tells us that human civilization could not have developed in any other pattern. The logic (a=b and b=c; therefore, a=c) says this is the irrefutable truth, whether we can independently prove it or not! Our archeological, climatological, and geological finds are only now beginning to bear all this out. However, the zodiac is a fantastic road map that we can absolutely rely on to see where we, as a people, came from and where we, as a living, global organism, are going in our future.

What we thought of as myth and legend is actually an illustrative, descriptive story of the human life cycle and the evolution of human civilization as a whole. The zodiac was created so we will know both our past and our future. It is an ancient message handed down through the ages. The zodiac is the story of us written in the stars so no one or any empire could ever change it...many have tried. As such, the zodiac tells the true story of us, not only as individuals, but as an entire human race. As below, so above. As above, so below.

PART THREE
THE AGE OF AQUARIUS

AQUARIUS

We have all heard that we are transitioning into the Age of Aquarius or are at the "dawning" of the Age of Aquarius. What does that mean?

There has been much argument and debate as to exactly when the change from the Age of Pisces to the Age of Aquarius was or will be. Some cultures, like the Mayan Indians, who measured the stars based upon the Winter Solstice instead of the Spring Equinox, calculated that the new age began at exactly 11:11am on December 21, 2012. That is why their old calendar ended on that date. To the Mayans, the end of the calendar did not signify the end of the world. It simply marked the end of an old age and the beginning of a new age, based upon their measurement of a change in the astrological alignments of the stars and planets on that date.

It was the Mayans who calculated the year to be 365.2422 days way back before technology. Their measurements calculated that the end of the old age and the beginning of a new age would be exactly 11:11am on December 21, 2012. For my money, I am going go with the Mayans and use 12/21/12 (numbers add up to 9) as the guesstimated start of the new Age of Aquarius.

There have been many other attempts to calculate the exact date of the change in ages from Pisces to Aquarius. Most involve using differing measuring points and/or differing calculation methods. According to some astronomers, we are already in the Age of Aquarius and to others, we will not be fully into the Age of Aquarius until some centuries from now. It all depends on what starting points and measurement techniques one uses. Perhaps exact measurements were never intended and should not be used.

Given that the constellations are not equal in size and given that there are gaps between some constellations and others appear to overlap, and given that there are various ways of measuring and calculating, it may not be possible to place an exact date when we will change to the Age of Aquarius. At this point, it is safe to say we are at least nearing a change in ages or beginning our transition from one age to the next.

The area of time surrounding a transition from one age to the next is known as the "cusp." Although astronomers disagree on almost everything except the "precession of the equinoxes," most would agree that we are at least on the cusp or nearing the cusp between the Age of Pisces and the Age of Aquarius. That is what it means to say that we are at the "dawning" of the Age of Aquarius, and this is where the Rainbow Generation fits into the bigger picture. More on that later.

There has been much speculation as to what changes will happen when we transition from the Age of Pisces to the Age of Aquarius. The ancient Greeks referred to the Age of Pisces as the "dark" age, with the Age of Aquarius to be an "age of enlightenment." Similarly, eastern astrology refers to the current age as the Kali Yuga or "iron" age with the new age to be a "golden" age of enlightenment called the Satya Yuga. It appears that both agree that the new age holds major changes for mankind...an age of enlightenment. But what does that mean? How will things change?

Perhaps it is better to measure the change in ages based upon the changes occurring in human civilization and its people. It is the change in human behavior and the change in our people that best signify the change in ages. In the 1960's the younger generation of that time announced a time when mankind would enter an age of enlightenment...a time when all manifestations of all colors, races and creeds would be welcome. They carried on in a mission to help usher in the new age to come.

The young people of the 1960's, dubbed themselves the "flower children," announcing the dawning of the Age of Aquarius. Tie-dye, flower-power, and love-ins became a recurrent theme. It became a fad for people to wear colorful clothing. It became fashionable to let your hair grow out, and people started wearing their hair longer and in all sorts of unconventional styles. People even decorated their homes in fantastic colors. I remember our family room having an orange theme, complete with an orange telephone. Our kitchen was multicolored, complete with olive green appliances and an olive-green telephone. We even had a pink telephone in our pink bathroom.

There was a popular song in the 1960's called "Aquarius" by the 5th Dimension, exalting the dawning of the new age. There is also a song called "Lay Down" by Melanie, reflecting on the meaning of Woodstock. I urge you to listen to these songs. Listen to the words! They show what the young people of the 1960's were experiencing and envisioning!

The people of the 1960's were announcing the coming of a new age, where all colors of the rainbow would be welcome…a time when humankind would change for the better. And, here we are, some 50 years later, that is starting to come true. We can see a significant change in our younger generations and the way we treat the Earth. We are seeing the beginning of a new age unfold, right before our very own eyes!

Simply put, entering the Age of Aquarius is the same for the whole human race as it is for the individual. It means, quite simply, that we as a human race are hitting middle age. To prove that, we simply need to look at current human behavior to see if we are, in fact, acting as if we are hitting middle age, as a people. Just as an individual hits a midlife crisis and then changes his or her ways and starts taking care of their bodies at the beginning of its Aquarius stage of life, the human race should be starting to change its ways and starting to care for Mother Earth, the body we all live on, if, in fact, we are entering the Age of Aquarius.

Although it started in the 1960's with the flower children, we are seeing more and more examples of humans worrying about our planet. We have come to the realization that if we do not take care of our planet, there may be no future for us, or there may be a future filled with even greater troubles. We have poisoned the air and waters. We have exploited natural resources, to the point of exhaustion and extinction. There are countless other examples of how human activity has and continues to hurt this planet and threaten our future, including global warming.

Over the last 50 years or so, we do see a growing effort to slow down the damage we are doing to this planet. We have started going green. We have started looking for renewable sources of fuel. We are recycling. We have enacted legislation and taken steps to stop water and air pollution and to slow down the exhaustion of certain natural resources. We see mankind, as a whole, starting to take care of this planet. Just as an individual hitting middle age must take care of his or her body if they want to continue to thrive and survive, we as a human race are starting to act as if we must take care of Mother Earth if we want to continue to thrive. Truly, mankind is hitting middle age, just as the zodiac predicted we would. Humankind, acting like we are the bearers of the waters of life on this planet, is proof to me that the Age of Aquarius is here!

We humans do indeed appear to be entering middle age. Not only are we starting to take care of this body (Mother Earth), we are also experiencing another tell-tale sign of middle age and that is called the "Midlife Crisis." This is a term we use to describe the angst, troubles, and unhappiness that forces us to change our ways at the beginning of middle age. Just as an individual goes through their midlife crisis sparking them to change their ways, this time for a healthier, more loving ethos, the entire human race is in the midst of its midlife crisis at this very time, requiring us to change as a human race to a healthier, more loving ethos.

    All one need do is turn on the news to learn of the long list of issues and other major troubles around the globe. These issues, including the current civil unrest in the U.S.A. and the pandemic, are sure signs that we are enduring our midlife crisis at this very time. The pandemic is teaching us that in the future, we need to be more careful and interact with each other in a healthier manner to prevent the spread of germs, viruses, and disease. The civil unrest tells us that we must change our ways. We need to stop celebrating hatred, bigotry, and racism. We need to clear the air of past doings and proceed in the future with a more positive, loving ethos. Although some only see doom and gloom, all should take heart. The zodiac tells us that there is a rainbow coming!

PART FOUR
WELCOME RAINBOW GENERATION

The constellation Aquarius is a man pouring water out of a pitcher. Not only is the water pouring out of the pitcher, almost every depiction of the Constellation Aquarius shows the falling water splashing. If one were to look up at the sun just before sunrise on the next Spring Equinox, using a cell phone app, one can see the sun's rays appear to be just beginning to shine through the splashing waters of the constellation Aquarius. This is significant!

What do you get when you shine sunlight through water droplets? You get a rainbow. The stars of the zodiac at this time are giving us the visual imagery of a coming rainbow. It foretells of a rainbow after the current storm. It foretells sunny days following the rains of the midlife crisis. But how can this be accomplished? How can we as a human race change our old ways and reinvent ourselves in a healthier, more loving ethos?

In order for a single human being to make it through their midlife crisis, they not only change their conduct, they create a whole new way of being. They change their entire ethos. If what we have learned thus far is true, then we should be seeing two things in our human civilization. First, the rainbow should be becoming more and more prevalent in our society at this time. Second, we should be seeing a material change in our children and in human society. I decided to look into it and found these things are happening, right before our very eyes!

First, we had the children of the 1960's, wearing every color of the rainbow, declaring the dawning of a new age. The young people of that generation, decked out in all colors, touted an age where all races, creeds, colors, persuasions, and manifestations would co-exist in harmony. "Make love, not war" was the mantra of the flower children. Although we may not have known it at the time, we flower children who were touting the coming of a new age, wearing and celebrating all colors, may have actually been foreshadowing the coming of a human rainbow!

I did not need to look long or hard to find many current examples of rainbow symbolism in our society at this time. I first turned to our television and radio for an afternoon and see if I see or hear anything about rainbows. Within one hour, I saw a television commercial, more than once, with the tag line, "Catch the rainbow!" I heard songs about the rainbow on the radio. One, a recent song, "Rainbow," and the other a remake of an older song, "Somewhere over the Rainbow." All within one hour.

I noted that the LBGTQ+ community has emerged and declared itself a welcome and permanent member of human society. The declaration of June as "Pride Month" is proof of that. They fly the rainbow flag! Just as the zodiac is foretelling the coming of a rainbow, the Rainbow Generation is emerging!

The final bit of research I did on rainbows was to see if there were any prophecies referencing the rainbow or the Rainbow Generation. Below are two prophecies I found:

There will come a day when people of all races,
colors and creeds will put aside their differences.
They will come together in love, joining hands in unification,
to heal the Earth and all Her children.
They will move over the Earth like a great
Whirling Rainbow, bringing peace, understanding
and healing everywhere they go.
(Navajo-Hopi Prophecy of the Whirling Rainbow)

When the Earth is dying
there shall arise a new tribe
of all colors and all creeds.
This tribe shall be called
The Warriors of the Rainbow
and it will put its faith in actions not words.
(Prophecy of the Native American Hopi people)

It is clear that rainbows are prevalent in our society at this time. I then decided to do a little research to see if there is a material change in our offspring at this time, and there is indeed a material change happening at this very time.

I came across several articles that addressed "indigo children." Among other things, I learned that in years past, humankind did not have any indigo in their auras (save for a special few), but that recent studies have revealed that almost all of our children now have indigo in their auras. An aura is the electromagnetic field that surrounds all living things. Each person's aura is like their own, unique, electromagnetic signature.

Having indigo in one's aura is significant for several reasons:

1. Children with indigo in their auras have traditionally been found to be wise beyond their years, like old souls, who may or may not also possess fantastic smarts, skills, talents, etc.

2. Indigo has been associated, in eastern practices, with the sixth chakra. Having indigo in your aura means that you now have the potential to open your "third eye"... "I am connected".

I am divine

I am connected

I am expressive

I am loved

I am strong

I am creative

I am safe

3. Having indigo in your aura means that your aura now contains all the colors of the rainbow, which are needed to potentially achieve the highest form of human consciousness.

Clearly the presence of indigo in our children's aura is an evolutionary advance in our children. There may even be some sort of DNA manifestation happening at this very time. Many insightful and enlightened people have been sensing a change in humanity happening all around them for years now. Hats off to all the old souls, light workers, and empaths out there. Your instincts are proving true. Keep up the good work! You will be dearly needed going forward! Your time has come!

[I noted in reviewing eastern practices, that once a person opens his or her third eye, only then do they have the potential to achieve the highest state of consciousness… "I am divine." I invite you all to read up on the volumes of literature on indigo children, the third eye, chakras, etc. It is fascinating, and there may be a connection between "humanity's road to enlightenment" and the changes in our children at this very time.]

In pondering the metaphysical and possibly physiological changes in our children, I noted that we older Pisceans were taught to think in an analog fashion (map). That is one of the reasons Pisceans are good at reading maps and putting things together such as modular furniture and model airplanes, etc. With the advent of the computer age, we have been training our children to think of things in a digital fashion (numbers and symbols). That is why Aquarians have trouble following maps and assembly instructions. However, where the analog system requires the following of a map to arrive at a conclusion, the younger generation simply needs to mentally open or close switches. They have been trained to analyze the world digitally since birth. They therefore analyze things differently and much faster than their Piscean elders. It also appears that these digital thinkers take to technology as if it were second nature to them.

The Rainbow Generation is the new "us." They are the first Aquarians. They are the first generation to be born to parents who were taught to think digitally. They are distinctly different from the Pisceans of the 1900's. And they are evolving faster and faster. Children of the same family, who are only years apart, are showing signs of being distinctly different than their older siblings. There seems to be a direct link between our children thinking digitally, the emergence of technology and the emergence of indigo in their auras. I leave it to our scientists to further explore the connection.

The change in our children is apparent, even to the casual observer. As I alluded to before, if you ever saw a two-year-old show their grandparents how to adjust "advanced settings" on their smartphones, or if you ever saw a four-year-old play concert piano, you are seeing with your own eyes that humankind is evolving rapidly.

The stars give us the visual imagery of a rainbow to come... and, arriving right on time, is the Rainbow Generation... manifesting at the dawning of a new age. A generation of children distinctly different from their predecessors, equipped and ready to heal this planet and carry us forward, through our mid-life crisis and into the golden Age of Aquarius. Seeing the bigger picture?

Just when the stars of the zodiac portend (foretell) the coming of a rainbow, the rainbow is manifesting here on Earth in the form of a new humanity. I believe the Rainbow Generation, and those that follow, may eventually form the Whirling Rainbow of Native American prophecy.

The Rainbow Generation manifesting on the Earth at this time is therefore no coincidence. It was foretold in the stars of the zodiac and in prophecy. They are here to heal this planet and its inhabitants. Their connection with each other extends beyond race, politics, religion, or national borders. Remember, indigo means, "I am connected." This new generation of humans has the ability to connect. Whether they know it or not, they have the ability to begin to unite this planet as one global living organism and begin to change all the bad things the Age of Pisces (the dark age) has left us with.

I believe that in the Age of Aquarius, more and more humans will all start to open their third eye, one at a time, and then, eventually, unite as one, just as the prophecies foretell. Only at that point can we reach the golden Age of Humanity! It may take many generations before we hit that golden age; however, the arrival of the Rainbow Generation means that we have begun humankind's next evolutionary leap. We are on our way towards the next Age of humankind! The future is unfolding right before our very eyes!

Now that we have filled up our planet, the biological drive to procreate is on sharp decline, as it should according to biological rules; however, the need and desire for love, connection, and individual expression, are rising rapidly. The Rainbow Generation, and all those who follow, will have increasingly more sensibilities, along with heightened understanding and compassion for each other and all living things. In the years to come, the Rainbow Generation will rule this world!

The Rainbow Generation is like one of many waves of Marines hitting the shores ahead of the rest, forcing change. They, as a generation, are recognizing that they have the power to affect sweeping changes in our society. A prime example is the recent, sweeping changes in how we treat animals. In just the last few years, it has finally become a felony to injure or neglect an animal. Circuses and sea world attractions are closing down as no one wants to see sentient beings caged, tortured, or held captive. Zoos are becoming more humane and animal friendly. There is a large push to adopt and rescue animals from shelters and to spay and neuter our pets. Humanity is finally beginning to show its humanity towards the defenseless animals we share this Earth with. We are showing love for other creatures. These are material changes that we are seeing, right in front of our eyes. These are only a few examples of many, however.

We are seeing young people invent whole new technologies and re-inventing older industries in ways older generations could only have dreamed of. It appears as if this new generation of young people are almost pre-programmed to see the world differently than the older generations do. It is as if they are proof of mankind's continuing evolution and development. We can only change the world, however, by first changing ourselves, and we are seeing that change, right in front of our very eyes, one child at a time.

Change is happening faster and faster; however, true change takes time. Just as you cannot stop the tide from coming in, you cannot force it to come in any faster than it will. All we can really do is help speed things up. By encouraging change and by sharing our thoughts, feelings, and hopes with each other, we can speed up the acceptance of the changes that lie ahead of us. Acceptance of our rainbow children is one such step. The sooner we can accept the changes in our own children, the sooner we can start to accept the changes that lie ahead for all of humankind. Our very survival depends on it.

The Age of Aquarius is going to present many difficult issues to be addressed for sure. We are now at our midlife crisis point as a human race. The current civil unrest and threats to Mother Earth are proof that we are in the midst of our midlife crisis. And there is more trouble ahead. However, the stars of the zodiac tell us a rainbow is coming. The Rainbow Generation and those that follow will be far better equipped to meet the challenges that lie ahead than their older Piscean forefathers and foremothers. The Rainbow Generation will help take us triumphantly into the new Age!

The generations that came before have left this world in critically bad shape with rising sea levels, global pollution, overpopulation, and lack of food and fresh water being major problems on the horizon. All of us, collectively, have a vital role to play in fixing these problems. The Rainbow Generation has manifested at this time to shape our future and preserve human life. It is just part of their nature. But they need all of our help, understanding, and encouragement.

Just like a man or woman at middle age must become the bearers of the waters of their own lives, the people who make up human civilization (the Rainbow Generation) will become the bearers of the waters of all life on this entire planet. It is the dawning of the Age of Aquarius, humanity's middle age, and the Rainbow Generation is here to help us take stock in ourselves and reinvent ourselves, this time with a healthier, more loving, ethos. Just an observation, however, it appears that love of life—all life—is the key to our survival in the challenges that lie ahead. Yes, as we keep hearing and seeing…love is the answer!

The Age of Aquarius is upon us, and it is the Rainbow Generation and those who follow that will take us triumphantly into this new age, just like a rainbow bridge over troubled waters. It was foretold in the stars. Please recognize that we are all part of a bigger picture. Do not wait. Start changing this world, today. How do you change the world? You start by changing yourselves. One step at a time. One person at a time.

If you want to see a cleaner world, then stop to pick up other people's trash and let others see you do it. If you want to see a more loving world, then start by holding the door open for the next person, or let someone ahead of you in line. Kindness is contagious and has a ripple effect. Make the world the kind, loving place you envision. It will take time, but things will slowly and continuously change in the direction you seek.

For those of you in the Rainbow Generation who are still unsure of yourselves, or your vital role in shaping the future of humankind, I leave you with the following words of encouragement:

COME OUT NOW CHILDREN AND HAVE NO FEAR
FOR THE ENLIGHTENED AGE OF MAN IS NEAR,
YOU DON'T FIT IN, NO REASON FOR WOE
YOU CAME TO CREATE A NEW STATUS QUO,
YOUR COMING FORETOLD IN THE STARS ABOVE
TO HEAL THIS PLANET THROUGH THE POWER OF LOVE,
YES, THE WATERS OF LIFE ARE YOURS TO BEAR
BUT YOU WILL SUCCEED SO DO NOT DESPAIR,
AND FOR YOUR TROUBLES THERE IS A PLUS
THE GOLDEN AGE OF AQUARIUS
AND FROM AQUARIAN LABORS WILL THEN BE BORNE
THE NEXT AGE OF MAN, CALLED CAPRICORN.
THIS IS OUR FATE, THIS MUCH I KNOW
LET US REJOICE, THE COMING RAINBOW!

Although my poem may sound corny, I urge you to read it again. It sums up the underlying message of this book! The coming rainbow is proof that humanity is going to be alright! We are going to make it through our midlife crisis! Imagine what glory days lie ahead for humankind, somewhere over the rainbow!

The zodiac truly is the revered Circle of Life! It not only celebrates all of the stages of an individual's life, the zodiac celebrates the stages in the development of the entire human race. Yes, my dear readers, the zodiac truly is the story of us! I rest my case!

EPILOGUE

Frequency and Humankind

My continued research on humanity led me to study frequency and its effects on people. It is my considered opinion that we cannot fully actualize as Aquarians (open our third eye as individuals and eventually as a human race) until sometime after we have changed our international audio frequency standard to A=432Hz. It is simple to accomplish and instrumental in the continued evolution of the human race!

Our scientists have uncovered that the natural resonant frequency of the universe is 432Hz (please note the numbers add up to 9). Not only that, scientists have discovered that music played at this frequency had a calming, relaxing effect on the listeners. Doctors who use music therapy to help patients, have found that music played at 432Hz yields the best results. You are invited to research the use of 432Hz in music therapy for Alzheimer's patients. As you will see, just as the type of music you listen to may affect your mood, the frequency at which the music is heard also has profound effects.

I also urge you to look at demonstrations that show how frequency affects sand patterns on metal plates. Frequency at A=432Hz (and fractions and multiples thereof) create beautiful and sometimes complex patterns, whereas other frequencies, like 440Hz, produce chaotic non-patterns. There are literally volumes of data on the beneficial effects of audio frequency at A=432Hz.

Currently, all of our audio is set to a frequency standard of A=440Hz. This standard was adopted by the United States in 1917, and then adopted internationally in 1953. When the standard was adopted, we did not have the technology we have today. We did not know that frequency could have such a profound effect on the listeners. We did not know that there are other frequencies which could be much more beneficial to the listeners.

Recent scientific experiments demonstrate that music played at 440Hz is more likely to reach our subconscious minds. The simple reason is that you are more likely to remember sound that is slightly out of sync and unconsciously controlled by it. Audio frequency at 440Hz strikes a node in our head, and we are therefore more likely to remember it or have it reach our subconscious minds.

Frequency at A=440Hz may be great for advertising products; however, scientific experiments show that sound at 440Hz actually puts man in more of an "uptight" frame of mind (Us vs. Them…very Piscean thinking). Music at 432Hz is natural and is soothing. Music soothes the savage beast. Think of music in a Japanese restaurant. That is music played at 432Hz. It is indeed relaxing and soothing.

When we have converted our global audio frequency standard to A=432Hz (remember that humankind is now a global organism), the listeners will be at a much more relaxed state, leading to greater tranquility amongst all the peoples. We urgently need to convert our audio frequency standard to A=432Hz as soon as can be arranged. Changing our frequency to be in sync with the natural resonant frequency of the universe will be a great benefit to mankind, and I believe will allow more and more individuals to eventually open their third eye, leading to the golden Age of Aquarius. It will go a long way to achieving global harmony, if nothing more. I truly believe that humankind will not be able to collectively open its third eye until some long time after we have changed audio frequency to 432Hz. Therefore, we need to act right away! The sooner we act, the better for all!

The agency that sets the audio frequency standard is the International Organization for Standardization (ISO). It is a multinational organization made up of governmental agencies and large corporations. Most of the corporate members benefit from advertising. They are not and never will be in favor of changing the frequency to a less rememberable one. Our young generation needs to step in and write to these agencies and corporations and get actively involved in changing our audio frequency standard to A=432Hz. I urge all my readers to get actively involved on this issue ASAP!

Write to the ISO, your legislators, and your congressmen and women; petition them and the Federal Communications Commission (FCC) and United Nations; get actively involved with the ISO and its member agencies and corporations and get our global audio frequency standard changed to A=432Hz. The sooner we do, the better for all of us, and the sooner we will achieve that "golden age"! I urge all of you to take action today! Our continued evolution as a human race depends on it! If I have taught you anything thus far, trust me on this! We need to align ourselves with the natural resonant frequency of the universe. Remember, Tesla, who concluded that, "It is all frequency!"

[I bet the ISO members will fight tooth and nail against changing the audio frequency standard to A=432Hz, and now you know why. The members benefit from keeping things the way they are: Mind controlled and ready to go at each other's throats on a moment's notice. Mark my words! We have a long and very important fight ahead of us on this issue! However, we must address this issue immediately, no ifs, ands, or buts! Perhaps the Rainbow Generation can unite the world under the banner of universal harmony and love, starting by getting us on the correct frequency standard!]

Patterns

What allowed me to decipher the zodiac is my ability to see patterns and connect dots, even when they are not clearly visible. One pattern that continues to catch my mind's eye, however, is a pattern involving our understanding of what we call "God."

With every change in Age, mankind's understanding of God has changed. Going as far back as the Age of Leo the Lion, after the we were hurt by pieces of the sun falling to Earth, God was seen as being like the sun, the ultimate giver of life and death who needed to be appeased to prevent it from harming us again. In the Ages that followed, God (or the gods) were seen as being entities that required worship and who may bless us or hurt us, if they so choose. In the Age of Taurus, we saw God with the temperament of a bull, who may not harm you, as long as you take care and rigidly follow the proper rules and practices. In the Age of Aries, God was seen as having the temperament of a ram, gently guiding and protecting his faithful flock. In the Age of Pisces, we came to see God as a loving father figure, who would protect you and could forgive you right up until your last breath.

What I notice is that with each passing Age, our understanding of God is becoming more and more forgiving and human-like. I think that part of the enlightening process in the Age of Aquarius is that humankind will once again change its understanding of God. I do not think humankind will invent something new. I think we will come to remember our earliest understanding of God. We will come to remember that we all, collectively, are the manifestation of God in this universe, time, place, dimension, whatever. We will collectively open our third eye, leading to the revelation that the divine resides within all things and all of us. "I am divine," leading to "We are divine!" Pantheism, if you will.

For those of you who do not believe in God (I do not see God as a Piscean father figure either), and for those of you who still do not believe there is a grand design to all of this, I leave you with the following:

We are all human. The word itself is actually one of the oldest words ever spoken or written. Its origins can be traced back to our oldest known language, Sanskrit. The word "human" is actually a combination of two Sanskrit words, "Om" and "Manu". The first word is "Om", pronounced, "Aum", means the "breath of god" in Sanskrit. The second word is "manu," which means "manifest." Therefore, the word "human" means "the breath of God manifest." God is in the very name we use to describe ourselves!

I believe that once we are fully in the Age of Aquarius, we, collectively, will come to remember that from the very beginning of humanity, we saw ourselves as "the breath of God manifested." We, collectively, are God's manifestation in this universe. As all the central figures in all our current religions have taught us, God is not "out there," God is "in here."

"Look inward." God is in each one of us, and each one of us is a god with the power to create or destroy life. Each one of us is a god with all the godlike responsibilities to care for each other and nurture and protect all life on this planet.

If we start to look at God this way, we will see a more secular understanding of God and our place in the universe. We will not look for a god or hero to come and save us. We will be fully comfortable being responsible for our own continued existence. We will be comfortable being the bearers of the waters of life on this planet. We will be comfortable with our god-like responsibilities. How would you treat other living things, if you were God, or better yet, you knew they were God?

I now understand the meaning of an ancient Hindu blessing, "Namaste"… "I bow to the divine within you." Let that sink in.

We, collectively, are one living creature…a human race, traveling through space on a spaceship called Earth. We must take care of (be the bearers of) the waters of life on this planet/spaceship if we want to continue to thrive. The sooner we start to unite as one, celebrating our differences, like crewmates on a spaceship, the sooner we can usher in the Golden Age of Humankind!

DEDICATION

I dedicate this book in three parts. First, I dedicate this book to the Rainbow Generation, who are proof to me that the Age of Aquarius is upon us!

Second, I dedicate this book to my loving and encouraging wife, family, and friends who have had to endure me talking about the zodiac over and over and over again, and again and again, on and on and on, obsessively, every single morning, noon, and night, uninterrupted, for years now, while I worked this all out in my head! Did I mention obsessively?

Lastly, I dedicate this book to all the humans who have ever lived. It is the sum total of all amassed knowledge and the sum total of the entire human experience that has allowed me to understand but a small fraction of what the Goddess Sophia showed me.

I can only hope that at least some of you can see the truth in what I have shared with you in this book for yourselves! I can only hope that this book may somehow help kick-start humankind on our road to enlightenment! I can only hope that I have at least started a conversation! Namaste!